LANDSCAPING WITH
tropical *plants*

By Monica Moran Brandies and the Editors of Sunset Books
Menlo Park, California

Creating a Tropical Paradise

Brilliant flowers and fabulous foliage colors are transforming gardens from Maine to San Diego. This book shows you how to get started creating your own tropical paradise. You'll also learn how to keep your garden alive, no matter what your climate.

For sharing their knowledge and experience, we extend thanks to Pam Baggett of Singing Springs Nursery in North Carolina, Mary Braunreiter of Boerner Botanical Gardens in Wisconsin, David A. Francko of Miami University in Ohio, and Rolfe Smith of Longwood Gardens in Pennsylvania; authors Richard R. Iversen, Susan A. Roth, and Dennis Schrader; and special consultant Jim McCausland.

Photographers

Monica Moran Brandies: 70B. Marion Brenner: 10; 74; 80. Lynne Brotchie—The Garden Picture Library: 62B. Rob Cardillo: 35MR; 62T. David Cavagnaro: 8L; 18L; 64; 85; 100R; 101TL; 109R; 112B. Van Chaplin/SPC Photo Collection: 88TR. Crandall & Crandall: 50R. Claire Curran: 58B; 63T; 71T; 107MR. Robin B. Cushman: 40R; 82T. Arnaud Descat/M.A.P.: 69TL; 99BR; 103T. Alan & Linda Detrick: 20R; 50L; 96T; 111T. David Dixon—The Garden Picture Library: 80B. Derek Fell: 2M; 11C; 18R; 22; 24TL; 25R; 26; 34TR, BL; 35TR, BL, BR; 37B; 38B; 40L; 41R; 42T; 43; 44TC, TR, MR; 55; 63B; 65; 66; 71B; 75R; 81B; 84L, C; 94TL; 97B; 119T. John Glover—The Garden Picture Library: 28R. Steven Gunther: 11R. Gil Hanley—The Garden Picture Library: 13; 32T. Jerry Harpur: 69TR. Larry Hodgson: 50R; 94BL, BR; 101TR. Saxon Holt: 24BR; 104B; 105TR. Dency Kane: 11L; 17; 93B; 108T. Charles Mann: 16B; 21BL; 119B. Jim McCausland: 77T. Meyer/Le Scanff—The Garden Picture Library: 21BR. Marie O'Hara—The Garden Picture Library: 48T. Jerry Pavia: 3M, B; 19L, R; 31T; 33T, BL; 36; 38MR; 39L, R; 44TL, ML, BL; 59; 72; 86; 88B, TL; 89; 90T, BL; 92; 93T; 95; 96BL, BR; 98; 99T; 100B; 101B; 102TR; 103B; 104TL, TR; 105B; 106; 107B; 108BL, BR; 109L; 110; 111B; 112T; 114TL, TR; 115T; 116T; 117T; 118; 121T. Howard Rice—The Garden Picture Library: 38T; 49T; 75L. Kate Zari Roberts—The Garden Picture Library: 30L; 42BL. Susan A. Roth: 2B; 3T; 6BR; 8R, 12; 15; 16T; 19C; 25L; 28L; 30C, R; 31B; 32B; 34TL; 37T; 39C; 46; 48B; 49B; 54; 58T; 60; 68; 77B; 78; 79; 81T, M; 82B; 83; 84R; 91B; 100T; 102TL, B; 105TL; 107T; 116B; 120; 121B. Christina Schmidhofer: 2T; 4. Richard Shiell: 9; 34BR; 97T. JS Sira—The Garden Picture Library: 1; 42BR. SPC Photo Collection: 20L; 24TR. Chad Slattery: 115B. Derek St. Romaine: 70T. Thomas J. Story: 67. Ron Sutherland—The Garden Picture Library: 40BC. Graeme Teague: 90BR. Michael S. Thompson: 44BR; 117B. Connie Toops: 91T. Mark Turner: 14T. Brian Vanden Brink: 69B. Deidra Walpole: 6L; 94TR. Rick Wetherbee: 6TR. Judy White/GardenPhotos.com: 14B; 25C; 114B. Ben Woolsey: 23. Steven Wooster—The Garden Picture Library: 33BR.

SUNSET BOOKS

VICE PRESIDENT, GENERAL MANAGER
Richard A. Smeby
VICE PRESIDENT, EDITORIAL DIRECTOR
Bob Doyle
PRODUCTION DIRECTOR
Lory Day
OPERATIONS DIRECTOR
Rosann Sutherland
RETAIL SALES DEVELOPMENT MANAGER
Linda Barker
EXECUTIVE EDITOR
Bridget Biscotti Bradley
ART DIRECTOR
Vasken Guiragossian

STAFF FOR THIS BOOK
MANAGING EDITOR
Susan Bryant Caron
SUNSET BOOKS SENIOR EDITOR
Marianne Lipanovich
WRITER
Monica Moran Brandies
DEVELOPMENTAL EDITOR
Barbara J. Braasch
COPY EDITOR
Elissa Rabellino
ADDITIONAL COPY EDITING
Rebecca LaBrum
ART DIRECTOR
Vasken Guiragossian
PHOTO EDITOR
Kimberly Parsons
ILLUSTRATOR
Jenny Speckels
ADDITIONAL ILLUSTRATIONS
Mimi Osborne, Erin O'Toole, Lucy Sargent
MAP DESIGN AND CARTOGRAPHY
Reineck & Reineck, San Francisco
PAGE PRODUCTION
Linda Bouchard
PREPRESS COORDINATOR
Eligio Hernandez
INDEXER
Ellen Davenport
PROOFREADER
Alicia Eckley

Cover: Photograph by Steven Gunther

10 9 8 7 6 5 4 3 2 1
First printing January 2004

For additional copies of *Landscaping with Tropical Plants* or any other Sunset book, call 1-800-526-5111 or visit us at *www.sunsetbooks.com*.

contents

The Tropical Allure **5**
*Why Grow Tropicals? ∾ Elements of a Tropical Garden ∾
Tropicals for Every Clime ∾ True Tropicals ∾ Tropical
Look-Alikes*

Designing with Tropical Flair **27**
*Elements of Design ∾ Color in the Garden ∾
Creating Effects*

Starting a Tropical Garden **47**
*Getting Started ∾ Adding New Tropicals ∾ Tropical Specialty
Nurseries*

Tropicals Under Cover **61**
Window Gardens ∾ Sunrooms and Greenhouses

Growing for Success **73**
A Spring Start ∾ Summer Maintenance ∾ Winter Care

A Tropical Sampler **87**
A to Z listings of treasured plants that are easy to find and grow

Index **127**

CHAPTER ONE

The Tropical Allure

TROPICALS ARE HOT! Their striking structural forms, masses of large leaves, flamboyant flowers, and lacy, finely cut foliage create a lush look evocative of Hawaii or Bali—a place far from home. And you can enjoy this luxuriant appeal no matter where you garden, thanks to less-tender tropical varieties being developed, the increasing availability of both true tropicals and hardier tropical look-alikes, and the practical ideas you'll find in this book. Botanical gardeners from Malaysia to Minnesota are designing fascinating tropical landscapes—and you can, too. ∾ Depending on where you live, you can landscape with tropicals in summer or year-round, on a small scale or a grand one. Amazing foliage, flowers, fragrance, and fun await—along with the special satisfaction that creative gardening gives. ∾ Your neighbors will be agog. Your garden may stop traffic—or even start a trend in the community.

Why Grow Tropicals?

If there's anything more exciting than setting out newly purchased plants in the garden, it's growing a brand-new kind of plant for a change of pace. And tropicals really do tend to stand out in most temperate gardens. They make striking focal points, and the foliage alone injects a punch of color and form that enlivens familiar-looking borders.

Because tropical plants grow so rapidly, they can quickly turn part of your yard into a secluded garden room. While you enjoy your hidden retreat, passersby may stop in their tracks to admire the view from the street. When you're in the mood, step out to share their wonder and, perhaps, take a little credit. Or peek through the foliage and enjoy their reactions unseen.

ABOVE: *Bromeliads capture the sun in a child's hideaway. Coleus, red ti plants, and the pink foliage of snow bush (Breynia nivosa 'Roseopicta') add bursts of color.* RIGHT: *Blooms of 'Jamaica Yellow' angel's trumpet (Brugmansia) hover above tropical sage (Salvia coccinea).* TOP RIGHT: *Gaudy 'Pretoria' canna provides privacy and a tropical feel.*

EXOTIC FLOWERS
AND FRAGRANCES

In their native outdoor habitats, tropicals bloom profusely, bearing large and showy flowers that evolved to attract pollinators such as insects, birds, and even mammals. Many blossoms exude the heady fragrances we associate with perfumes; ylang-ylang, for instance, is more familiar to us as Chanel No. 5! Even a few containers of such exotic plants can turn an ordinary garden into a fragrant showplace.

Since day length and temperature change little with seasons near the equator, tropical plants typically bloom over a long period—and some, like pentas, are in flower every day of the year. Because they need not race to set seed, individual blossoms last longer, too, so their sensational performance in your garden is not a one-day matinee but a long-running show.

Pick your colors—from the soft pastels and satiny whites of jasmine and moonflower (*Ipomoea alba*) to the fiery brights of red-hot poker to the intense hues of chocolate cosmos.

7

DRAMATIC FOLIAGE

Tropical foliage is easily as astounding as tropical flowers—and just as varied, offering myriad shapes, textures, and colors. Rain forest natives tend to have large, flat, glossy leaves (like bananas), to shed the constant moisture, or lacy ones (like ferns and palms), to let it pass through. Denizens of the tropical desert, on the other hand, have thick, succulent stems and leaves to store water; some of these have a hairy or thorny coat that provides some small measure of shade. Leaves also offer rich textures, from the smooth, shiny leaves of bromeliads through the puckered, quilted foliage of many begonias to the feltlike softness of purple velvet plant *(Gynura aurantiaca)*. And the color range of foliage is astonishing—just consider the maroons, corals, pinks, and near-blacks of coleus, one of the tropical plants that adapt to gardens countrywide.

BELOW LEFT: *Brilliant 'Burgundy Giant' fountain grass* (Pennisetum) *and 'Mr. Wonderful' coleus create a blended backdrop for licorice plant* (Helichrysum petiolare) *and verbena 'Tapien Lavender'.* BELOW RIGHT: *Against a background of broad leaves, the fronds of a cinnamon fern—both stiff fertile fronds and finely cut nonfertile ones—stand out sharply, illustrating the dramatic impact of contrast.*

A GLOBAL OUTLOOK

Botanists on plant-hunting safaris, as well as gardeners on vacation, have always been excited by the exotic plants they see abroad. The beauty of tropicals inspires travelers, making them eager to create that same lush look in a cooler climate.

Happily, this goal isn't hard to achieve—and once you've grown these plants yourself, you'll feel more at home abroad when you see them in their native habitats. You'll discover that many tropicals are far more than ornamental; they're used for food, drink, building material, and much more. Passion fruit, for example, makes a potent punch; bamboo provides both fuel and furniture; and aloe and cardinal flower have medicinal properties.

What if you never make it to Indonesia or Hawaii, Brazil or Bali? Movies, books, and television can acquaint you with countries you may never visit— but growing plants from those lands will bring you even closer, adding a whole new dimension to your life. Admiring a towering banana tree or inhaling the sweet perfume of a gardenia in your own garden lets you experience the beauty, warmth, and exuberant growth that people in the tropics take for granted.

ABOVE: *The intricate blossoms of passion vine* (Passiflora) *come in many sizes and many shades of lavender; one flaunts bright red petals. The plant grows like a weed in warm climates, but it's almost too beautiful to pull up. Butterflies love it in or out of bloom.*

RIGHT: *Bamboo offers hundreds of choices—and almost as many uses.*

Elements of a Tropical Garden

A dense canopy of greenery, large and rustling leaves, bizarre and brilliant flowers that perfume the air…if the flamboyance of a tropical garden makes you yearn for exotic locales, you don't need to board a plane. You can have your own little rain forest outside all summer, and then move it indoors in winter.

LUXURIANT GROWTH FROM TOP TO BOTTOM

Although seemingly random in arrangement, tropical gardens are carefully composed for contrast in colors and textures. Still, the overall feeling is one of wild abundance, unusual form, and incredible, jungly density. Against a backdrop of tall trees and shrubs, vines drape a mantle of color; more vines carpet the ground with flowers. Some tropical plants spring up to the height of a small tree in a single season; others fill in at various levels right down to the ground. Not one square foot is left bare or without interest.

DAZZLING FOLIAGE, FLOWERS, AND FRUIT

A tropical garden gains most of its constant color from foliage. In much of the country, colorful leaves appear with the first warmth of spring and persist all the way until the first autumn chill. And the palette goes far beyond the many shades of green found in the usual temperate-climate landscape, encompassing greens marbled and streaked with white, yellow, and cream, and solid colors and combinations of burgundy, red, yellow, pink, purple, blue, and silver. Such brilliance has even more impact when the leaves are tropically large: Think about variegated elephant's ear, red banana leaves, and gaudily striped canna foliage.

Against this already vivid background, tropicals burst with blooms arresting in both color and form—in a show that can run all season long or come in waves spanning weeks or even months. And in some tropicals, eye-catching bracts provide color and fragrance long after the actual flowers have come and gone.

Besides the usual flower spires and rounded heads, you'll find many more fanciful shapes—butterflies, lobster claws, raindrops. Colors run the gamut from soft to intense. Your garden can glow with vibrant blankets of bougainvillea, fantastically shaped gingers and bromeliads in

Big-leafed plants create a tropical look. Many of these bold beauties are thirsty; where water is scarce, focus on palms and other more drought-tolerant choices, like this castor bean.

Caladium bicolor   Hedychium gardnerianum   *Pineapple*

jewel tones, and striking bird of paradise, with blooms that seem ready to take wing from their perch on the stem.

Some of the blossoms you'll enjoy are surprisingly familiar; one of the most colorful tropicals, for example, is the common nasturtium, a native of South and Central America that can cover the ground, climb to a roofline, or fill a vase with brightness.

Though only a few tropicals will bear fruit in cooler climates, the mere possibility is exciting—and the plants are worth growing even if you never harvest a crop. The luckiest gardeners will enjoy a whole new world of taste and fascinating form. The banana infloresence changes from day to day, with dark red sheaths dropping away to reveal bunch after bunch of smooth, small bananas and blossoms as the stem stretches and bends under the weight. The pineapple fruit is an aggregate of flowers that bloom at the tip of each little "knob" on the skin. And figs hide their blooms inside the fruit, so you never see them.

What Are Tropical Plants?

Strictly speaking, true tropicals originate just north and south of the equator, from the Tropic of Cancer (in the north) to the Tropic of Capricorn (in the south). Including much of Africa, South and Central America, India, Indochina, the Caribbean, and the South Pacific, this region contains by far the largest number of plants in the world. The consistently warm climate allows for year-round vigorous growth.

Though true tropicals vary greatly, most thrive on heat and humidity. They don't tolerate freezing temperatures, and some can't even withstand temperatures in the 40s. But gardeners can work around this by growing the truly equatorial plants as annuals, using more cold-hardy varieties, and planting tropical lookalikes that have a greater tolerance for chilly conditions.

More frost tolerant than true tropicals are subtropical plants, native to regions bordering the true tropics—anywhere from 300 to 700 miles to the north or south, wherever citrus will grow. If a freeze kills the tops of these plants, the roots may still survive.

Tropic of Cancer
15° N

Equator

15° S
Tropic of Capricorn

True tropical plants are native to the hot, humid latitudes on either side of the equator, within the zone defined by the Tropic of Cancer (at about 23° north) and the Tropic of Capricorn (at about 23° south)—from Havana to Rio de Janeiro.

A WATERY WORLD

Water is as essential to a tropical garden as plants are. Pools and ponds offer places for water lilies to grow and sites to encircle with wetland plants—and they reflect and expand their surroundings, making the garden seem larger and more mysterious. Water features can be anything from a half-barrel "pool" to a professionally installed landscape centerpiece with goldfish or koi to add color. Even so simple a detail as a birdbath centered with a flat stone acts as a magnet for butterflies and birds, offering them a place to alight and drink while adding flashing colors to an already brilliant scene.

Birds will also be drawn by the sound of a splashing fountain—and humans will be entranced by it. Fountains need not be complicated; you can easily make your own from a sunken 5-gallon bucket with a screened cover topped by a copper bubbler. Or choose from the wide variety of fountains available at home and garden centers.

Tropical gardens look as natural around swimming pools and spas as they do bordering tropical beaches, providing a lush backdrop that makes swimming and soaking more fun. Add a colorful canopy, a changing-room tent, or even a palm-thatched roof over a picnic table, and you have an ideal outdoor retreat.

Whether a natural wetland (top, designed by Heronswood Nursery in Kingston, Washington) or only a small fountain (bottom, at Chanticleer in Wayne, Pennsylvania), water features make fascinating focal points.

GARDEN ART AND ACCENTS

While plants are the stars in a tropical setting, garden art and accents set the scene and add a personal touch. One gardener collects tiled stepping-stones to match her plantings—some decorated with butterflies for a butterfly garden, others adorned with orchids for a more exotic section. Another gardener sets copper figures of dragonflies amid the greenery to welcome these transient visitors; still another uses weathered stone statuary to create the feel of an ancient sanctuary in a jungle clearing.

In tropical landscapes, as in gardens of any style, a simple path and bench put people in the picture, transforming the space into an outdoor room where we feel comfortable enough to sit and rest. A birdhouse or bird feeder, a gazing ball on a pedestal, tiki lights that lengthen our stay beyond dusk on a soft summer night—all add to the relaxing, inviting feel.

And don't forget trellises and arbors, classic accents that play several roles: Besides supporting lush tropical vines, they create "doorways" that welcome guests and provide shade.

A stone lantern accents a garden.

Microclimates Make the Difference

Some garden spots are more protected than others: pockets where two walls meet; courtyards; south-facing walls, where heat is absorbed throughout the day and slowly reflected through the night; and areas beside fences or windbreaks. Temperatures also stay a bit warmer near a brick chimney or a black asphalt drive.

In warm climates, the shade of evergreens helps hold in heat that would otherwise be radiated outward. Many tropical plants that flower best in full sun survive well in light shade.

Water holds heat, too, so areas immediately around a pool or larger body of water are safer than open-ground spots for marginal plants. The coldest places are open spots to the north and east of structures, and at the bottom of a hill, where cold air pools.

Wind is also a factor to consider in choosing planting locations. It will shred large leaves, such as those of bananas. A slightly tattered look does no harm as long as it's not extreme—but too much wind can render foliage both unattractive and unhealthy.

Cold air moves downhill and collects on the north side of a house (left). The south side stays warmer (right), where the heat from the sun is absorbed throughout the day by the house wall and bare soil, and is slowly reflected back onto the plants overnight.

Cold air collects

Cold air drains

13

Tropicals for Every Clime

*No matter where you live, you can grow tropicals outdoors when-
ever night temperatures typically remain above 55°F/13°C. And
it's possible to enjoy many of these plants year-round by moving
them to a sunroom, sunny window, enclosed porch, or greenhouse in winter (see "Tropicals under Cover," pages 61–71).*

HAWAII

The only truly tropical state in the U.S. has a climate ideal for both people and plants. With no worries about winter cold, gardeners who live below 2,000 feet there can plant and enjoy any tropical all year, watching it grow and mature from year to year until it reaches its natural size. In Hawaii's cooler zone (from 2,000 to 6,000 feet), some tropicals (like coconut palms) can't handle the cool nights; stick with those that have some cold resistance.

FLORIDA AND THE GULF COAST

Tropical plants grow and bloom right into (and sometimes through) the winter, unless they're nipped back by frost or killed down to the roots by a freeze. If a long or hard freeze threatens, you'll need to move the least hardy plants indoors, cover them with burlap or sheets, or take cuttings and start the plants over again.

Even in a warm winter, some tropicals stop growing when temperatures dip into the 40s. They can look pretty bleak for

ABOVE LEFT: *Bougainvillea cascades over a wall with date palm* (Phoenix) *and holly fern* (Arachniodes simplicior) *in a Gulf Coast garden.*
LEFT: *This secret garden in Key West features several kinds of palms. Other plants—some chosen for foliage, others for flowers—provide a layered look and a feeling of abundance.*

Prickly pear cactus (Opuntia) *has a tropical look and comes in a range of sizes. It's hardy in many climates and flourishes with little or no watering.*

a while, but growth will start again with the first warm weather and speed up when summer rains begin. Other plants may melt away in the wet heat, but most true tropicals love it!

THE SOUTHWEST

The arid southwestern states have generally long, hot, dry summers; desiccating spring winds; and both winter and summer rainy seasons (especially as you move west). Low-elevation regions from Phoenix to California's Imperial and Coachella valleys rarely freeze in winter, so subtropicals thrive there. The intermediate- and high-elevation parts of the South-

west get regular killing frosts and occasional snow. Put the emphasis on hardy subtropicals there; grow true tropicals as annuals or in containers that you bring into a sunroom in winter. When plants are outside, keep them well watered and sheltered from wind.

COASTAL SOUTHERN CALIFORNIA

In the relatively mild, humid climate west of the mountains, gardeners grow a vast array of tropicals and subtropicals. All they need for success is regular watering and protection from the howling, desert-dry Santa Ana winds of fall and winter.

NEW ENGLAND, THE NORTHERN TIER OF STATES, AND THE ROCKY MOUNTAINS

From New England south to New York and Pennsylvania, and west all the way to eastern Washington, summers still get hot. The farther north you live, the shorter the warm growing season; and the farther west you get, the more arid the climate and the more severe the winds. Landscaping with tropicals is still possible, however, even if you only accent your planting with a few exotics in containers that you can move indoors or into a greenhouse for nurturing over the winter. In the Rockies, summers are mild and the growing

season short, but the intense light really brings out tropical colors. Aridity and hail can be a problem there; grow plants in containers, give them overhead shelter, and water regularly.

THE PACIFIC NORTHWEST

Ocean currents keep this region fairly cool in the summer and fairly mild in the winter. Most of the rain comes in fall through spring, leaving summers on the dry side and plants in need of regular watering. Cool summer days and nights limit the growth of many true tropicals, but gardeners can still get a convincing tropical look with combinations of ferns, hot-colored perennials, large-foliaged plants, and broadleafed evergreens, such as bamboo and rhododendrons.

ABOVE: *Tropical look-alikes form this garden's backbone, combining well with true tropicals to extend the summertime show.*

LEFT: *Bring it outdoors in summer, indoors in winter—a tropical garden-in-a-pot fits anywhere.*

Purple-leafed cannas contrast with bright coleus and the dark foliage of ornamental sweet potato.

NORTHERN CALIFORNIA

Like the Pacific Northwest, coastal Northern California has relatively cool summers and mild winters. The Central Valley also has mild winters, but its hot summers help many tropicals to bloom lavishly and ripen fruit. Neither the coast nor the interior gets much summer rain, so you'll need to give moisture-loving tropicals more regular water. The farther south you live, the more your choices lean toward those in Southern California and the Southwest.

THE MIDWEST

The hotter and more humid the summer, the more extensive your choices, the less you'll need to water, and the longer your growing season—but there are tropicals for drier areas as well. In the western part of this region, wind and hail are big issues; give tropicals shelter there with windbreaks.

THE SOUTHEAST

The growing season is even longer there, the winters shorter, and rainfall more abundant, so raising tropicals is easy and rewarding. Botanical gardens, universities, and nurseries in this region are growing ever more tropicals with ever greater success. You can, too.

True Tropicals

From the myriad of tropical plants, we picked some of the most dramatic, colorful, and bountifully blooming. Some are familiar, others more exotic, and all adapt well to more temperate climates.

Using tropical plants in temperate climates isn't a new idea: They were featured in European gardens as far back as the 1800s. That round bed of cannas in the front yard— a popular detail of Southern California gardens in the 50s— harks back to the formal botanical gardens of Victorian days. In fact, many tropicals made the move from their native lands to Florida and Southern California long ago.

Today, however, gardeners all over the country are discovering tropicals. Increased demand and advances in plant breeding are producing ever larger numbers of improved cultivars with greater hardiness, more intensely colored foliage, and more dazzling flowers. The resulting landscapes are like fireworks displays, bursting with color and beauty—not just for minutes but for months.

Tropicals Grown as Annuals

Many of the most colorful annuals, among them impatiens, portulaca, coleus, caladium, and a number of salvias, are tropical perennials (as are a few shrubs and vines) that have become standard choices for bedding plants in every garden—in cold-winter climes as well as in the warmest, close-to-tropical areas. Dozens of other selections, such as hyacinth bean and *Alternanthera* gain in popularity every year. You'll typically have to start these from seed or cuttings, though you may be lucky enough to find some of them as plants.

ANNUAL BEDDING PLANTS
YOU CAN BUY ANYWHERE
Amaranth *(Amaranthus)*
Amethyst flower *(Browallia)*
Black-eyed Susan vine *(Thunbergia alata)*
Blackfoot daisy *(Melampodium leucanthum)*
Busy Lizzie *(Impatiens walleriana)*
Caladium bicolor

Chocolate cosmos *(Cosmos atrosanguineus)*
Cockscomb *(Celosia)*
Coleus × hybridus
***Dahlia* hybrids**
Floss flower *(Ageratum houstonianum)*
Nasturtium *(Tropaeolum majus)*
Pepper *(Capsicum)*
Rose moss *(Portulaca)*
Sage *(Salvia,* some)
Spider flower *(Cleome hasslerana)*
Star clusters *(Pentas lanceolata)*
Wishbone flower *(Torenia fournieri)*

ANNUAL POSSIBILITIES TO START
FROM SEED, CUTTINGS, OR BULBS
Alternanthera
Butterfly lily *(Hedychium coronarium)*
Castor bean *(Ricinus communis)*
Coral vine *(Antigonon leptopus)*
Hyacinth bean *(Dolichos lablab)*
Mexican sunflower *(Tithonia rotundifolia)*
***Thunbergia,* some**

LEFT: *'Carmencita Bright Red' castor bean, 'Silver White' mealycup sage* (Salvia farinacea), *and 'Inferno Red' begonia.* RIGHT: *Amaranths grow over a longer season and get larger in the tropics.*

Other Easy-to-Grow Tropicals

These are perennials, vines, shrubs, or small trees in their native lands—and enjoyed as permanent plants where climate permits. In cooler climates, they're grown as annuals or protected during winter.

PERENNIALS

Agave

Banana *(Musa)*

Begonia, some

Bird of paradise *(Strelitzia reginae)*

Bloodleaf *(Iresine herbstii)*

Bromeliads *(Aechmea, Billbergia, Cryptanthus, Guzmania, Neoregelia)*

Canna **hybrids**

Crinum

Elephant's ear *(Alocasia, Colocasia esculenta)*

Firecracker flower *(Crossandra infundibuliformis)*

Gingers *(Alpinia, Costus, Zingiber officinale)*

Kalanchoe

Orchids *(Cattleya, Phalaenopsis)*

Polka-dot plant *(Hypoestes phyllostachya)*

Snake plant *(Sansevieria trifasciata)*

Sweet potato, ornamental *(Ipomoea batatas)*

Tradescantia

Zebra plant *(Aphelandra squarrosa)*

SHRUBS OR SMALL TREES

Allamanda, some

Caricature plant *(Graptophyllum pictum)*

Chenille plant *(Acalypha hispida)*

Chinese hibiscus *(Hibiscus rosa-sinensis)*

Croton *(Codiaeum variegatum 'Pictum')*

Dracaena, some

Fiddleleaf fig *(Ficus lyrata)*

Gardenia augusta

Persian shield *(Strobilanthes dyerianus)*

Philippine violet *(Barleria cristata)*

Princess flower *(Tibouchina urvilleana)*

Rubber tree *(Ficus elastica)*

Shrimp plant *(Justicia brandegeeana)*

Ti plant *(Cordyline fruticosa)*

Rhododendron, Vireya group

Yellow shrimp plant *(Pachystachys lutea)*

VINES

Bougainvillea

Canary bird flower *(Tropaeolum peregrinum)*

Cup-of-gold vine *(Solandra maxima)*

Glorybower *(Clerodendrum,* some)

Jasmine *(Jasminum,* many)

Mandevilla **hybrids,** some

Philodendron scandens

Queen's wreath *(Petrea volubilis)*

Split-leaf philodendron *(Monstera deliciosa)*

Wax flower *(Hoya carnosa)*

Ti and yellow shrimp plants brighten a partly shaded area.

Colorful croton and caricature plant contrast with palm and ginger.
Design: Carlos Godoy

Beehive ginger (Zingiber spectabile) goes dormant in winter.

Tropical Look–Alikes

Just as exciting as true tropicals are hardier tropical look-alikes. Some of them are members of genera that also include natives of the tropics (see "Cold-Hardy Cousins," page 22); others simply have that tropical look.

All these plants create stunning landscapes—and as a plus, they tolerate winters in cooler climates, making them a practical choice for gardens. The degree of cold hardiness varies considerably among the plants in the following photos, descriptions, and lists; check the encyclopedia (page 87) or consult a good nursery to see where they thrive. By selecting the hardiest cultivars and the most protected sites, adventurous gardeners often succeed in growing these beauties one or even two zones to the north of the norm.

Any plant with large or showy foliage can fall into this class: purple- or copper-leafed coral bells, larger-leafed hostas, *Ligularia,* and sedum. Those with flamboyant flowers, such as Joe Pye weed and red-hot poker, qualify as well. All of these plants look gorgeous in tropical settings, even if they are "impostors." Gardeners in warmer climates would love to grow some of these look-alikes—but can't!

LEFT: *A luxuriant tropical garden at the entrance to this charming house offers visitors a warm welcome. A tall banana overlooks the lawn's edging of bright impatiens and caladiums, and potted sago palms (Cycas revoluta) on the porch focus attention on the brick walkway and inviting entry.*

ABOVE: *Vividly striped foliage of 'Pretoria' canna and leaves of castor bean are big and bold, standing out against red fountain grass (Penni-setum setaceum 'Rubrum'), orange Mexican sunflower, and low purple floss flower.*

FAR LEFT: *Red-hot poker.*

LEFT: Ligularia stenocephala *'The Rocket'.*

21

Cold-Hardy Cousins

More than a few tropical families have a cold-hardy cousin or two in the bunch. *Hibiscus rosa-sinensis* (Chinese hibiscus) may thrive in Tahiti, but *H. syriacus* (rose of Sharon) is covered with only slightly smaller flowers from summer to frost, and it survives winters of –10°F/–23°C or below in Iowa, summers of blistering heat and heavy rain in central Florida, and every gradation in between. Gardeners in much of the country can also grow the native *H. moscheutos* (rose-mallow), which bears foot-wide flowers from late summer until frost. The yuccas soapweed *(Yucca glauca)* and Adam's needle *(Y. filamentosa)* are hardy perennials in northern states. The smaller, bushier angel's trumpets *(Datura* species, such as *D. innoxia* and *D. metel)* will grow from seed to shrub very quickly, producing upraised, fragrant trumpets that open in the evening. Grown as annuals in cooler states, they self-sow without being invasive. And though many bamboos are tropical and subtropical, some are hardy to 0°F/–18°C, and a few will even tolerate –20°F/–29°C.

In the palm family, perhaps 100 of the more than 1,500 species will flourish where temperatures drop to 20°F/–7°C; some will survive below 0°F/–18°C. The native saw palmetto *(Serenoa repens)* grows wild as far north as the coast of Virginia and west into Arkansas. By paying special attention to winter protection, gardeners can grow cold-hardy palms farther north than most people imagine, and even up into the mildest parts of southern Canada.

To some, the Southern magnolia *(Magnolia grandiflora)* is even more a signature tree of the South than the palm. Breeders have developed more than 100 cultivars, and the hardiest of these, such as 'Bracken's Brown Beauty' and 'Edith Bogue', withstand temperatures below 0°F/–18°C with the help of careful siting, wind screens, antidesiccant sprays, and winter watering.

Southern Belle rose-mallow brings a touch of the tropics to temperate gardens. A shrubby perennial, it produces huge blooms from early summer to frost.

Trees with a Tropical Touch

These trees will be attention grabbers in your garden. Some have brilliant foliage or flowers; others feature strikingly large leaves; still others have lacy foliage that creates a nice contrast to large leaves, such as those of bananas. They vary in hardiness, so check in the encyclopedia or with a good local nursery before you make your selections.

Angelica tree *(Aralia elata)*
Black locust *(Robinia pseudoacacia)*
Common catalpa *(Catalpa bignonioides)*
Crape myrtle *(Lagerstroemia indica)*
Edible fig *(Ficus carica)*
Empress tree *(Paulownia tomentosa)*

Goldenchain tree *(Laburnum × watereri)*
Goldenrain tree *(Koelreuteria paniculata)*
Japanese pagoda tree *(Sophora japonica)*
Red buckeye *(Aesculus pavia)*
Red horsechestnut *(Aesculus × carnea, red-flowered cultivars)*
Silk tree *(Albizia julibrissin)*
Smoke tree *(Cotinus coggygria)*
Sourwood *(Oxydendrum arboreum)*
Southern magnolia *(Magnolia grandiflora cultivars)*

Empress tree, banana, and 'Little Gem' magnolia form a canopy above blue wheatgrass (Agropyron) *and lace-cap hydrangeas.*

Shrubs with an Exotic Look

Shrubs like those listed below can become the background and backbone of a tropical garden.

Anise tree *(Illicium,* **some)**
Butterfly bush *(Buddleja)*
Camellia
Carolina jessamine *(Gelsemium sempervirens)*
Euonymus, some
Heavenly bamboo *(Nandina domestica)*

Holly-leaf osmanthus *(Osmanthus heterophyllus)*
Hydrangea
Indigo bush *(Indigofera kirilowii)*
Japanese aralia *(Fatsia japonica)*
Japanese aucuba *(Aucuba japonica)*
Leatherleaf viburnum *(Viburnum rhytidophyllum)*
Lily-of-the-valley shrub *(Pieris japonica)*
Oregon grape *(Mahonia aquifolium)*
Rhododendron **(hardy evergreens only)**
Rose of Sharon *(Hibiscus syriacus)*
Staghorn sumac *(Rhus typhina)*

Butterfly bush (Buddleja davidii) *brings movement to the garden.*

Bright caladiums ring the lawn of this Florida home; tall leatherleaf viburnums shade the comfortable lawn furniture.

Vines for a Jungle Feeling

Nothing can weave fragrance and flowers through a garden like a vine; and out of season, the serpentine trunks of some still have the exotic, tropical look of strangler figs. Best of all, most are fairly fast growers.

Common trumpet creeper *(Campsis radicans)*
Crossvine *(Bignonia capreolata)*
Japanese honeysuckle *(Lonicera japonica)*
Japanese wisteria, Chinese wisteria *(Wisteria floribunda, W. sinensis)*
Kiwi *(Actinidia kolomikta)*

The ornamental kiwi is grown for its fabulous foliage, but females also bear fruit.

Tropical–Looking Perennials

Many of these plants are already familiar to gardeners in temperate climes. Using a special cultivar with variegated or richly colored foliage adds tropical appeal.

LOW-GROWING (UP TO 2 FEET)
Big blue lily turf *(Liriope muscari)*
Coral bells *(Heuchera,* **many with**
decorative foliage)
Euphorbia polychroma
Five-finger fern *(Adiantum aleuticum)*
Hardy begonia *(Begonia grandis)*
Heartleaf bergenia *(Bergenia cordifolia)*
Plantain lily *(Hosta,* **some)**
Rhubarb *(Rheum × hybridum)*
Sedum spectabile
Wood fern *(Dryopteris,* **some)**

MEDIUM HEIGHT (UP TO 4 FEET)
Alstroemeria aurea
Beard tongue *(Penstemon digitalis)*
Bear's breech *(Acanthus mollis)*
Cardinal flower *(Lobelia cardinalis)*

Cast-iron plant *(Aspidistra elatior)*
Dahlia
Goldie's wood fern *(Dryopteris goldiana)*
Horsetail *(Equisetum hyemale)*
Indian rhubarb *(Darmera peltata)*
Japanese coltsfoot *(Petasites japonicus)*
Ligularia
Montbretia *(Crocosmia × crocosmiiflora)*
Red-hot poker *(Kniphofia* **hybrids)**
Sea holly *(Eryngium,* **some)**
Soapweed *(Yucca glauca)*

TALL (ABOVE 4 FEET)
Adam's needle *(Yucca filamentosa)*
Bugbane *(Cimicifuga)*
Cinnamon fern, royal fern *(Osmunda*
cinnamomea, O. regalis)
Eulalia *(Miscanthus sinensis)*
Gunnera tinctoria
Joe Pye weed *(Eupatorium purpureum)*
Plume poppy *(Macleaya cordata)*
Rose-mallow *(Hibiscus moscheutos)*
Tasmanian tree fern *(Dicksonia antarctica)*
Texas star *(Hibiscus coccineus)*

Large-leafed hostas such as H. sieboldiana 'Elegans' have the look of true tropicals. Design: Landcraft Environments

With its bright dinner plate-size blooms, 'Babylon' dahlia is a scene-stealer in any garden.

Easy-to-grow plume poppy (Macleaya cordata) has large, silvery leaves and fragrant flowers.

CHAPTER TWO

Designing with Tropical Flair

CREATING A BEAUTIFUL GARDEN *is like sewing a quilt or decorating a room. You visualize how the project will look when completed, then decide what materials you'll need to put it together. Having a design in mind—or, better yet, on paper—can keep you focused. Making important decisions in the planning stage prevents expensive mistakes in the buying stage, as well as extra labor in the planting process—after all, moving plants in your mind or erasing them on a sketch is a lot easier than transplanting them.*

❧ In this chapter we'll discuss some of the elements involved in designing a tropical garden. To help you along, we have included photos and illustrations showing how a number of gardeners have achieved dramatic effects by dreaming up a great plan and then choosing the plants to make that dream a vivid reality.

Elements of Design

To make a picture—or a garden—pleasing to the eye, it takes the ability to visualize the finished piece. And when your "paints" are living, growing plants, it's vital to know your subjects well.

Because plants change from season to season, from day to day, or even from hour to hour as sunlight falls on them and then retreats, designing can be complex. It's an art as well as a craft.

Still, certain basic elements always apply: Plant form and size, color schemes, and the use of contrasts and focal points are factors to consider when planning a garden anywhere, in any style or size. You might want to start small, blending tropicals into your existing garden by adding one or two carefully placed exotic houseplants during warm weather or filling containers with eye-catching annuals

ABOVE: *Even water-wise planting can create a tropical paradise. A century plant makes a powerful focal point; bougainvillea vines add bright color.*

LEFT: *This cool-climate garden features fantastic foliage: variegated rubber tree, elephant's ear, canna, and bloodleaf.*

chosen to complement the landscape around them. Chances are good, though, that these small tropical touches will inspire other, more extensive plans.

Any garden evolves over time; using tropical plants just speeds up the process. You can change and improve the look of a garden quickly—sometimes even in a single day!—by rearranging plants for a more vivid display or replacing poor performers with bolder show-offs. Forget the old saying "The first season plants tend to sleep, the second to creep, the third to leap." Carefully selected tropicals and tropical lookalikes leap into growth right from the start. And those that last over a winter will grow even faster and larger in the second and successive seasons.

CHOOSING PLANTS FOR SIZE AND FORM

Setting plants close together gives that feeling of wild tropical abundance, but you still need to leave each plant enough room to develop and show off its natural beauty. Don't let size be a surprise! Check the encyclopedia to see how tall and broad the plants you choose are likely to become, bearing in mind that they'll be larger under ideal conditions, and be smaller and grow more slowly in cooler areas where the growing season is shorter (or when they're confined in containers).

Think about size and shape when deciding just where to position different plants, too. As a general rule, if your tropical retreat will be viewed from one side only, place taller, straighter plants in the back and shorter, more rounded ones in front; if it will be seen from all sides, position the tall growers in the center. A banana, for instance, will grow high enough that you can plant something low in front of it without obscuring the fountain of arching leaves at its top—but a 3- to 5-foot firecracker plant has blossoms that cascade almost to the ground, so it should be displayed more in the foreground.

Plants with big, flamboyant foliage need plenty of room to spread, but there's often room beneath their large leaves to show off lower-growing plants. Try placing shade-loving annuals or smaller-leafed perennials there, or fill the space with tropicals in containers that can be moved as needed. For spring interest, you can enjoy pansies or early-blooming bulbs in these areas;

LEFT: *Traveler's tree's giant leaves accent a tropical garden.* CENTER: *The foliage of a castor bean towers above other plantings.* RIGHT: *Canna,* Phormium, *coleus, salvia, and elephant's ear give a garden the look of a jungle. Design: Landcraft Environments*

bulbs in pots are easy to bring in, and then remove to a sunny, out-of-the-way spot to die down naturally after they've finished flowering. When large-leafed shrubs themselves provide all the cool-weather color you want, you can simply mulch beneath them until it's warm enough to plant tender tropicals.

Consider accents and camouflage, as well—position plants to play up what you want to emphasize, or locate them where they will screen what you'd rather conceal.

CREATING CONTRASTS WITH FOLIAGE

Fascinating foliage is often a tropical plant's main selling point, so always keep leaf size, texture, shape, and color in mind. For the most interesting picture, combine large, paddle-shaped leaves with thin, spiky foliage; contrast broad, flat leaves with fine, feathery ones, or shiny foliage with matte, leathery leaves. Variegated and colored foliage adds even more impact.

Remember that a plant's foliage may change color with maturity. A croton's leaves turn from green to red, for example, while most other plants have brighter (often brilliant) new growth that may mature into softer colors or turn green.

Amount of sunlight can also affect foliage color—so you may be able to use the same plant for both brighter and more muted effects, depending on whether you place it in sun or shade.

RIGHT: *An agave cultivar stands out against a backdrop of fern and bamboo.*
BELOW: *Fronds of Tasmanian tree fern* (Dicksonia antarctica) *arch over palm grass* (Setaria palmifolia) *and Japanese anemone* (Anemone × hybrida). *Design: Benjamin J. Hammontree*

The Magic of Repetition

As your eye travels around the garden, it welcomes echoes of color and form, especially in a landscape bursting with brilliant hues and striking silhouettes. Repeating a leaf shape, flower shape, or color tends to organize and harmonize, producing a feeling of pattern rather than clutter. Echoes in form or color also create focal points—the low, fountainlike leaves of lily turf *(Liriope)* in front of tall, arching sugar cane foliage, for example, or the dark red leaves of a massive Abyssinian banana emphasizing the purple foliage of a nearby 'Black Magic' elephant's ear *(Colocasia esculenta).*

LEFT: Grasses in the foreground echo the vaselike form of banana leaves and the texture of palms; colorful coleus plants call attention to the path.

BELOW: The color of the large Persian shield leaves is repeated by purple princess flower; zinnias bloom in front. Design: Landcraft Environments

32

MAXIMIZING FLORAL DISPLAY

Use contrasts to accent the shape, size, and color of blossoms, too. For instance, setting off spires of salvia or cat whiskers with rounded masses of nasturtiums or wishbone flowers *(Torenia fournieri)* calls attention to both low- and tall-growing plants. Weeping angel's trumpet *(Brugmansia),* with pendent flaring flowers 8 to 12 inches long and 6 inches across, is always a scene-stealer, but letting the blooms sway above the stiff blossoms of bromeliads, the starry clusters of pentas, or the colorful foliage of ti plants sets them off still more.

If your summers aren't long enough for treelike angel's trumpets, grow the shrubbier types *(Datura)* as annuals, letting their upraised trumpets welcome the night, while spikes of scarlet sage or weeping arches of amaranths *(Amaranthus)* draw the eye away from the fading trumpets in the morning. Combine iridescent yellow allamanda blooms with deep

TOP: *Impatiens repeat the hue of bougainvillea, while a banana adds tropical flair behind a great burst of color.*
LEFT: *The pink flowers of wax begonia 'Cocktail Brandy' echo the colors of coleus 'Japanese Giant'. Both varieties bloom constantly until the first frost.*
ABOVE: *Amaranth,* Nicotiana, *stonecrop, castor bean, and dahlias form a red band in front of a dramatic green* Phormium.

blue plumbago or purple Brazilian sky flower *(Duranta stenostachya);* or echo the allamanda's color with yellow-flowered lantana or gold-variegated foliage such as that of 'Pretoria' canna.

EMPHASIZING FRAGRANCE

Place aromatic-foliaged plants like lantana where you'll brush against them in passing, releasing the scent; or locate them close to a garden bench, where you can rub a leaf between your fingers and enjoy the perfume. Try to put scented flowers high enough so that you can easily sink your nose into them; add a few sweet-smelling choices

to raised containers. The flowers of a pine cone ginger should be close enough to a pathway to squeeze each time you pass: they yield a lanolinlike lotion that feels and smells delightful when rubbed on hands and face.

TOP LEFT: *Nothing fills the garden with evening-to-morning fragrance like the gorgeous blossoms of an angel's trumpet* (Brugmansia).

TOP RIGHT: *Scented leaves of some geraniums* (Pelargonium) *evoke fragrant memories.*

ABOVE: *The foliage of lantana exudes a warm, herbal scent.*

BOTTOM LEFT: *Angel's trumpet produces hundreds of fragrant blooms.*

Tropicals with Fabulous Flowers

Most of these plants also have fantastic shapes and sizes; those marked with an asterisk bear the brightest flowers.

Amaryllis *(Hippeastrum)*
Angel's trumpet *(Brugmansia)*★
Banana *(Musa)*
Bird of paradise *(Strelitzia reginae)*★
Bougainvillea★
Bromeliads *(Aechmea, Billbergia, Cryptanthus, Guzmania, Neoregelia)*★
Candle bush *(Senna alata)*
Canna hybrids
Cat whiskers *(Orthosiphon stamenius)*
Frangipani *(Plumeria)*
Ginger lily *(Hedychium)*
Ginger, true *(Zingiber officinale)*
Gold vein plant *(Sanchezia speciosa)*★
Hibiscus★
Lobster-claw *(Heliconia)*★
Lotus *(Nelumbo,* most)
Magnolia, many★
Mandevilla★
Mexican flame vine *(Senecio confusus)*★
Moonflower *(Ipomoea alba)*
Passion vine *(Passiflora)*★
Pentas lanceolata★
Princess flower *(Tibouchina urvilleana)*★
Rose-mallow *(Hibiscus moscheutos)*
Salvia, many★
Shell ginger *(Alpinia zerumbet)*★
Solanum, some
Spathe flower *(Anthurium)*★
Thorn apple *(Datura)*★
Thunbergia, some

Bright, bold blooms compete for attention in many ways. Above, amaryllis features a bouquet per stem. At left, shade-loving spathe flower's heart-shaped bracts look almost artificial. Stunning rose-mallow 'Lord Baltimore' blossoms, bottom left, reach a foot across. Lobster-claw, below, flaunts blazing, long-lasting color.

35

Color in the Garden

When you're growing tropicals, it's hard not to have a colorful garden! Almost all of these plants provide color with their flowers, fruit, foliage, or bark, and even the many shades of green make a good contribution as a background for other colors. For variety in color throughout the seasons, try rotating showy plants like begonias, bromeliads, and orchids.

It's ideal, of course, to see a plant in bloom before deciding where to locate it in the landscape, but often your only preview will be a photo in a catalog or reference book. Whenever you can, though, try to see the plant growing in a botanical garden. Take a camera and notebook with you to capture colors and record names of varieties or cultivars. Note any striking color combinations you'd like to duplicate.

Because a tropical garden is rearranged often (annually in cooler climes), keep notes on blossom and foliage colors and pleasing color combinations as the growing season progresses. These notes will help you duplicate and expand on your successes— and avoid repeating mistakes.

WINNING WAYS WITH COLOR

The skillful use of color can give the garden a feeling of openness or make it seem smaller and more intimate. On the color wheel (shown below), cool colors are grouped on the right side of the wheel, and warm colors are

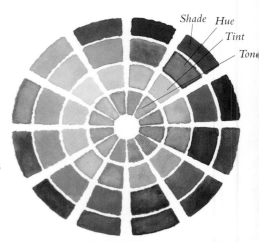

Shade Hue Tint Tone

ABOVE: *'Pretoria' cannas, 'Radiation' lantana, and grand Datura 'Yellow Ruffles' paint a sunny garden canvas. Design: Landcraft Environments*

LEFT: *This combination of yellow allamanda and purple bougainvillea is a fine example of contrasting colors.*

RIGHT: *African daisies and zinnias pick up the colors of coleus.*

on the left. Because cool colors (especially blue) retreat visually, they give the impression of space and are best viewed close up or against a background of white or a warm color. Warm colors, on the other hand, seem to surge forward, making them ideal for accents or focal points.

MONOCHROMATIC A monochromatic color scheme—one that uses many different shades of one color—unites a garden while still including enough variation to keep things from looking flat. As always, choose a range of plant forms and foliage textures and shapes to make the scene more interesting.

HARMONIOUS For a livelier look, select harmonious hues: those that lie between two primary colors on the color wheel. For example, if a plant has red blossoms that lean toward orange, you can enhance it with other flowers and leaves in shades ranging from red through orange to yellow. Red blooms that are on the purplish side will look wonderful combined with colors that cover the range from red through violet shades to blue.

CONTRASTING You may also want to use contrasting colors—those lying opposite each other on the color wheel, such as yellow and violet or red and green. (In fact, nature often chooses this sort of scheme for you, combining contrasting hues in the same plant— red blossoms against green leaves, for instance.)

When juxtaposing such warm and cool colors, remember that it takes much more of the cool color to balance the warm and keep it from demanding all the attention.

Don't overlook white and gray plants. They go well with everything, brightening some combinations and softening others.

Tropicals with Colorful Foliage

These plants all offer constant color from spring to fall, with only subtle changes. Most, such as coleus, take on a deeper, brighter color in more light; a few, like snow bush and some elephant's ears, will revert to green if the shade is too deep. Many (coleus and Persian shield are two examples) benefit from frequent pruning, since the new growth is most colorful; use the prunings in bouquets to admire indoors.

In the following list, we sometimes suggest particularly vivid selections—but in many cases you have lots of options within a genus or among selections of a single species. Check the possibilities at your favorite nursery, or look through catalogs or Web sites (see page 59).

Abyssinian banana, red-leafed
   (*Ensete ventricosum* 'Maurelii')
Acalypha
African daisy *(Osteospermum)*
Alternanthera
Angel's trumpet (*Brugmansia* 'Variegata')
Banana (*Musa*, some)
Bougainvillea
Caladium bicolor
Canna hybrids, some
Caricature plant *(Graptophyllum pictum)*
Century plant *(Agave americana)*
Cigar plant (*Cuphea ignea* 'Variegata')
Coleus × *hybridus*
Creeping fig (*Ficus pumila* 'Variegata')
Crinum, some

Croton (*Codiaeum variegatum* 'Pictum')
Elephant's ear (*Alocasia, Colocasia,* some)
Elephant's ear *(Xanthosoma sagittifolium)*
Euphorbia, some
Flowering maple (*Abutilon*, some)
Gardenia augusta 'Radicans Variegata'
Gold vein plant *(Sanchezia speciosa)*
Golden creeping daisy (*Wedelia trilobata*
   'Outenreath Gold')
Hibiscus, some
Indian coral tree *(Erythrina variegata)*
Kalanchoe pumila
Persian shield *(Strobilanthes dyeranus)*
Pineapple flower *(Eucomis bicolor)*
Pine cone ginger (*Zingiber zerumbet*
   'Variegata')
Plectranthus, some
Potato vine (*Solanum jasminoides*
   'Variegata')
Pseuderanthemum atropurpureum
Purple velvet plant *(Gynura aurantiaca)*
Red pineapple (*Ananas bracteatus*, some)
Rubber tree (*Ficus elastica*, some)
Shell ginger *(Alpinia zerumbet)*
Silver vase *(Aechmea fasciata)*
Sky flower (*Duranta erecta* 'Variegata')
Snow bush *(Breynia nivosa)*
Spathe flower *(Anthurium crystallinum)*
Sweet potato, ornamental *(Ipomoea batatas)*
Ti plant *(Cordyline fruticosa)*
Tillandsia, some
Tradescantia
Umbrella plant *(Cyperus alternifolius)*
Wood sorrel *(Oxalis vulcanicola)*

Crotons   'Red King Humbert' canna   African mask elephant's ear
                                                    (Alocasia × amazonica)

Creating Effects

Showy tropicals and the right accessories can be dramatic accents in any garden. Whether you want to add a punch of color to a green border, wake up a humdrum area with a sculptural specimen plant, or create a textured privacy screen or an exotic retreat with a South Seas feeling, you'll find plants that will achieve the desired effect.

FOCAL POINTS

Some tropical plants are so striking in size, shape, or color that they make natural focal points, drawing the eye to wherever they are—in the curve of a path, near a bench, at an overlook beside a pool. These brazen beauties stand out sharply among less dramatic plants, adding depth and variety to a garden.

Select focal-point plants carefully for a satisfying composition. You want them to pop out from the surrounding landscape—trees, shrubs, and perennials—yet blend smoothly with other architectural accents, such as wood carvings, weathered benches, and sculpted poles.

Having too many focal points disrupts the serenity of a garden, so it's sometimes better to group them; put a couple of striking tropicals next to an attractive bench, for example. This way, you'll create one strong focal point instead of distracting the eye of the viewer with several weaker ones.

Striking focal points punctuate a garden scene, adding variety and directing the viewer's eye. At left, bird's nest fern (Asplenium nidus) contrasts nicely with a large tree fern and smaller, blue-green foliage. At right, pots of agave enliven a planting of geraniums (Pelargonium), licorice plant, and succulents.

ABOVE: *Wild exuberance characterizes a tropical garden. Silver-blue agave echo and brighten the seating area.*

LEFT: *The layered, jungle look behind a quiet garden seat includes* butterfly bush (Buddleja), *St. Johnswort* (Hypericum), *and* stonecrop (Sedum spectabile). *Design: Liz Deck*

A LAYERED LOOK

In the tropics plants fill every part of the landscape, from ground to treetops. You can duplicate this wild look in your garden with a lush, free-flowing design of exotic plants in many shapes and sizes. Position shade-tolerant types (there are many) under trees, eaves, and awnings; plant sun lovers where they'll get maximum light.

Away from existing trees, annual giants such as Mexican sunflower *(Tithonia rotundifolia)* and castor bean grow tall in a single season. Let vines add yet more layers of greenery and color as they trail along the ground or climb through nearby trees and shrubs.

Architectural Tropical Plants

Plants with commanding presence make a strong visual impression. Use them individually or in small groups, either in interesting containers or in the ground.

Abyssinian banana *(Ensete ventricosum)*
Agave
Bamboo *(Bambusa, Fargesia, Phyllostachys)*
Bamboo palm *(Chamaedorea seifrizii)*
Bird of paradise *(Strelitzia reginae)*
Blushing bromeliad *(Neoregelia carolinae)*
Bronze dracaena *(Cordyline australis* 'Atropurpurea')
Coral fountain *(Russelia equisetiformis)*
Crinum, **many**
Cycads *(Cycas revoluta, Dioon, Zamia fischeri)*
Date palm *(Phoenix)*

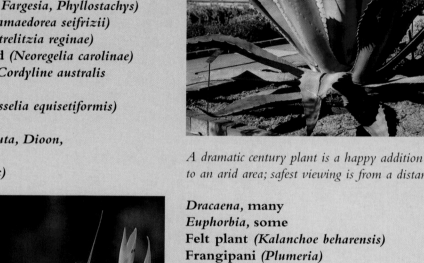

A dramatic century plant is a happy addition to an arid area; safest viewing is from a distance.

Dracaena, **many**
Euphorbia, **some**
Felt plant *(Kalanchoe beharensis)*
Frangipani *(Plumeria)*
Ginger lily *(Hedychium)*
Lady palm *(Rhapis excelsa)*
Lemon grass *(Cymbopogon citratus)*
Lobster-claw *(Heliconia)*
Maternity plant *(Kalanchoe daigremontiana)*
Needle palm *(Rhapidophyllum hystrix)*
New Zealand flax *(Phormium tenax)*
Palm
Papyrus *(Cyperus papyrus)*
Queen palm *(Syagrus romanzoffianum)*
Queen's tears *(Billbergia nutans)*
Red fountain grass *(Pennisetum setaceum* 'Rubrum')
Red pineapple *(Ananas bracteatus)*
Shell ginger *(Alpinia zerumbet)*
Silver vase *(Aechmea fasciata)*
Snake plant *(Sansevieria trifasciata)*
Spiral flag *(Costus spiralis)*
Staghorn fern *(Platycerium bifurcatum)*
Sugar cane *(Saccharum officinarum)*
Ti plant *(Cordyline fruticosa)*
Traveler's tree *(Ravenala madagascariensis)*
Tree fern *(Blechnum, some)*

LEFT: *A tree fern spreads fronds above a garden sculpture.*

RIGHT: *Bright bird of paradise flowers resemble birds about to take flight.*

Tropical-Looking Vines and Vinelike Plants

Vines are important for a layered look. They are great climbing into trees and shrubs, blanketing branches, and trailing their flowers to the ground—but if you want a neater appearance, provide a trellis, pergola, or other support for them. Many of the blooming sorts put on a show in summer; to bring color to your garden over a longer season, combine them with a woody plant that blooms fairly early in the year, such as a wisteria, forsythia, or rose. Single asterisks indicate sprawling, scrambling shrubs that can be trained or supported to grow as vines; double asterisks mark plants that do well cascading over the edge of a container.

Allamanda
Aristolochia
Bougainvillea★
Cape plumbago *(Plumbago auriculata)*★

Clerodendrum × speciosum, C. thomsoniae
Creeping fig *(Ficus pumila)*
Flowering maple *(Abutilon)*★
Grape ivy *(Cissus)*
Ipomoea
Jasmine (*Jasminum,* **many**)
Licorice plant *(Helichrysum petiolare)*★★
Mandevilla, **many**
Mexican flame vine *(Senecio confusus)*
Orchid vine *(Stigmaphyllon ciliatum)*
Passion vine *(Passiflora)*
Periwinkle *(Vinca major)*★★
Philodendron, **some**
Potato vine *(Solanum jasminoides)*
Pothos *(Epipremnum pinnatum* **'Aureum')**
Purple velvet plant *(Gynura aurantiaca)*★★
Snail vine *(Vigna caracalla)*
Thunbergia, **most**

A lush drape of bougainvillea sets off the white flowers of Nerium oleander.

Plants with Dramatic Foliage

Standouts because of their fantastic foliage, these plants give any garden a tropical touch. Some are succulents; others have large leaves with a bold outline or very long compound leaves with many smaller leaflets.

Abyssinian banana *(Ensete ventricosum)*
Agave
Banana *(Musa)*
Begonia
Bird of paradise *(Strelitzia reginae)*
Caladium bicolor
Candle bush *(Senna alata)*

Canna **hybrids**
Castor bean *(Ricinus communis)*
Chinese yellow banana *(Musella lasiocarpa)*
Elephant's ear *(Alocasia, Colocasia esculenta)*
Elephant's ear *(Xanthosoma sagittifolium)*
Eucharist lily *(Eucharis × grandiflora)*
Fiddleleaf fig *(Ficus lyrata)*
Ginger lily *(Hedychium)*
Gold vein plant *(Sanchezia speciosa)*
Lobster-claw *(Heliconia)*
Naranjilla *(Solanum quitoense)*
Philodendron, **many**
Pine cone ginger *(Zingiber zerumbet)*
Rubber tree *(Ficus elastica)*
Spiral flag *(Costus spiralis)*

Caladium bicolor   Bromeliads, philodendron   Variegated agave

Small-Leafed Tropicals for Contrast

These small-leafed plants create a fine-textured complement to larger-leafed sorts.

African daisy *(Osteospermum)*
Bloodleaf *(Iresine herbstii, I. lindenii)*
Citrus, some
Ferns, most
Licorice plant *(Helichrysum petiolare)*
Ornamental grasses, many
Plectranthus, **some**
Sky flower *(Duranta erecta)*
Solanum pyracanthum
Sweet potato, ornamental *(Ipomoea batatas)*
Tradescantia, **some**
Wood sorrel *(Oxalis vulcanicola)*

CLOCKWISE FROM TOP RIGHT: Pteris cretica, Miscanthus sinensis, *bloodleaf, licorice plant.*

Tropic Tempo

Neon-brilliant reds, oranges, and yellows are tempered with splashes of dark blue and purple in a tropical tapestry so vivid it virtually vibrates. Even the dominant foliage plants—canna and New Zealand flax—carry out the bright, hot theme. The planting is long and fairly narrow, suitable for a spot at the front of a garden or along a walkway, where it's certain to grab any passerby's attention. It is at its blazing best from late spring through summer.

Plant List

A. **New Zealand flax** (*Phormium* 'Maori Chief')
B. *Rosa* 'Charisma'
C. *Canna*
D. **Blue marguerite** (*Felicia amelloides*)
E. **Border penstemon** (*Penstemon × gloxinioides*)
F. **Mexican hat** (*Ratibida columnifera*)
G. **Daylily** (*Hemerocallis*, red cultivar)
H. **Daylily** (*Hemerocallis*, orange cultivar)
I. **Daylily** (*Hemerocallis*, yellow cultivar)
J. **Lily-of-the-Nile** (*Agapanthus*)
K. *Coreopsis grandiflora*
L. **Threadleaf coreopsis** (*Coreopsis verticillata*)
M. **Blanket flower** (*Gaillardia × grandiflora*)
N. **Trailing African daisy** (*Osteospermum fruticosum*)
O. **Moss verbena** (*Verbena pulchella gracilior*)

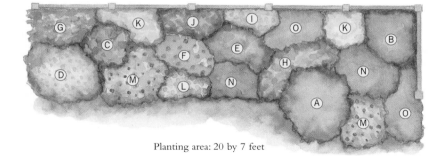

Planting area: 20 by 7 feet

CHAPTER THREE

Starting a Tropical Garden

THE GOOD NEWS IS that you know more about tropical plants than you suspect. Just look around your house—those houseplants that grace your windowsills and add colorful accents to living areas and sunrooms are probably tropicals or subtropicals. If moved outside during a warm summer growing season, they can jump-start a garden, quickly adding grandiose greenery and brilliant color. ∾ *This chapter takes a look at introducing tropical houseplants to their natural habitat, where to place them for the best results, and what exciting effects you can anticipate as they grow in their new environment. It also explains how to add other tropical vegetation through seeds, cuttings, layering, and visits to specialty nurseries and gardens.*

Design: Litdle & Lewis Inc.

Getting Started

Moving tropical houseplants outside in summer when nightly temperatures climb above 55°F/13°C gives them a whole new lease on life. Plants that struggled to stay alive in dry indoor heat suddenly begin to thrive. Pests that plagued stressed plants disappear with gentle washing by garden hose and summer rain. Moderate temperature fluctuations and higher humidity aid rapid plant growth.

CLIMATE AND PLANT BEHAVIOR

A tropical plant's growth pattern is affected dramatically by the length and warmth of the growing season and summer temperatures. Once you are aware of this, you can use it to your advantage and enjoy a greater variety in the space available.

During a long, warm growing season, flowering plants like aloe and begonia quickly set buds and then burst into blossoms much more abundant than those you have seen indoors. As they climb, pothos and philodendron exchange their familiar small, heart-shaped foliage for much larger leaves with deeply cut margins and holes. Species of the coral tree *(Erythrina)* that grow as tall as 45 feet in Hawaii thrive as deciduous shrubs in Southern California and become perennials in the Southeast, though they may die back in winter.

TOP: *Passion vine* (Passiflora), *ivy* (Hedera), *and geranium* (Pelargonium) *move outdoors easily.* RIGHT: *A mandevilla vine cascades across the eulalia* (Miscanthus sinensis) *toward an agave and a bromeliad* (Aechmea). *Design: Kevin J. Doyle*

Need Indoor Plants?

Favorite indoor plants, including paradise palm *(Howea forsteriana)* and Boston fern *(Nephrolepis exaltata* 'Bostoniensis'), appreciate time outdoors, growing larger, greener, and fuller for their next stint at indoor decoration. But moving all your houseplants outdoors for a summer sojourn can leave your home looking bare. As an alternative, keep thriving plants indoors, taking out only those that obviously need Mother Nature's magic wand. When inside plants look a little limp, switch them with plants that have benefited from their time outdoors. You can also take cuttings of plants to increase your stock indoors and out (see page 56). To become known as a tropical plant expert, simply share extra plants with others.

Cannas, coleus, ornamental sweet potatoes (Ipomoea batatas), red fountain grass (Pennisetum setaceum 'Rubrum'), and dahlias thrive in their containers. Design: Scott Arboretum

MOVING PLANTS OUTDOORS

To start acclimating houseplants to a new environment, set them outdoors for a few hours on warm spring days. Choose a shady spot that is well protected from the wind. If space is an issue, you can group containers, stacking smaller pots on the soil surfaces of larger ones.

Groom plants by removing any dead foliage and pruning as needed. Save any prunings you may want to turn into cuttings (see page 56). Then wash plants well with a hose. If a plant shows signs of insect infestation, wash it with soapy water (dishwashing soap works well), making sure you reach the undersides of leaves and the crotches of petioles and stems.

By late afternoon, when you move plants back inside, they will have a new lease on life. The more time that plants spend outside, the larger they grow and the more accustomed they become to this new, brighter, more humid environment.

Houseplants That Thrive Outdoors

Here is a sampling of houseplants that can move outdoors in summer to start your tropical garden.

Amaryllis *(Hippeastrum)*
Anthurium
Asparagus, ornamental *(Asparagus)*
Begonia
Bromeliads *(Aechmea, Billbergia, Cryptanthus, Guzmania, Neoregelia)*
Aloe
Cacti and succulents
Chinese evergreen *(Aglaonema modestum)*
Corn plant *(Dracaena fragrans)*
Croton *(Codiaeum variegatum* **'Pictum')**
Dumb cane *(Dieffenbachia)*
Euphorbia
Ferns

Fiddleleaf fig *(Ficus lyrata)*
Norfolk Island pine *(Araucaria heterophylla)*
Orchids
Palms
Peace lily *(Spathiphyllum wallisii)*
Peacock plant *(Calathea makoyana)*
Philodendron
Pothos *(Epipremnum pinnatum* **'Aureum')**
Prayer plant *(Maranta leuconeura)*
Purple velvet plant *(Gynura aurantiaca)*
Rubber tree *(Ficus elastica)*
Schefflera
Snake plant *(Sansevieria trifasciata)*
Spider plant *(Chlorophytum comosum)*
Split-leaf philodendron *(Monstera deliciosa)*
Ti plant *(Cordyline fruticosa)*
Wandering Jew *(Tradescantia fluminensis, T. zebrina)*
Zebra plant *(Aphelandra squarrosa)*

LEFT: *Peace lily prefers low light indoors, shade outside.* ABOVE: *Angel-wing is one of many begonias that bloom easily on a summer porch.*

Planting area:
20 by 7 feet

Plant List

A. *Philodendron scandens*

B. Rubber tree *(Ficus elastica)*

C. Ti plant *(Cordyline fruticosa)*

D. Cascade palm *(Chamaedorea cataractarum)*

E. Coleus *(Coleus × hybridus)*

F. Corn plant *(Dracaena fragrans)*

G. *Begonia*

H. Wishbone flower *(Torenia fournieri)*

I. Hawaiian elf schefflera *(Schefflera arboricola)*

J. Dumb cane *(Dieffenbachia maculata)*

K. *Philodendron bipinnatifidum*

L. Norfolk Island pine *(Araucaria heterophylla)*

M. Pothos *(Epipremnum pinnatum 'Aureum')*

N. *Aphelandra squarrosa*

O. Snake plant *(Sansevieria trifasciata)*

P. Croton *(Codiaeum variegatum 'Pictum')*

Q. Busy Lizzie *(Impatiens walleriana)*

R. Wandering Jew *(Tradescantia fluminensis)*

S. Maidenhair fern *(Adiantum raddianum),* **spider plant** *(Chlorophytum comosum),* **rat's tail cactus** *(Aporocactus flagelliformis),* **lady of the night** *(Brassavola nodosa)*

Houseplants on Summer Vacation

Under a tree or around a bench, foliage houseplants take on new life that will amaze you all summer and into the autumn. Some, like begonias, will bloom with bright colors. Some will climb the trunk of the tree that shades them. Orchids and bromeliads will set buds for winter bloom, or bloom even sooner. And if that snake plant blooms in September, bring it back indoors in the evening, when it has a heavenly fragrance. Add a few annuals that are actually tropicals (see page 18) for color.

Sun-Loving Houseplants Around a Garden Light

Take those aloes out into the sun (gradually, of course), and they are sure to spread and likely to bloom. Put other succulents and cacti in planters, hang them from a post, and surround it all with the bright, jewel colors of nasturtiums.

1. **Stonecrop** *(Sedum kamtschaticum)*
2. **Rat's tail cactus**
   (Aporocactus flagelliformis)
3. **Medicinal aloe** *(Aloe vera)*
4. **Garden nasturtium**
   (Tropaeolum majus)

HARDENING OFF

The term "hardening off" simply means gradually getting plants adjusted to new conditions. A change in environment is a shock to any plant's system. When plants move outdoors, they have to cope with variations in light, temperature, and wind—all conditions that can damage tender foliage. However, there is less stress on tropical plants because you keep them indoors until night temperatures are above 55°F/13°C.

Even so, start the adjustment for indoor plants by gradually reducing the amount of water you give them to begin toughening their tissues. Move them out on a warm, cloudy afternoon for an hour or two.

There are three ways to harden off plants: (1) Place pots in a protected spot for an hour or so, gradually increasing the stay for 7 to 10 days; (2) move pots to a protected site for a day or so, and gradually transfer them to less protected sites; (3) move pots directly to permanent locations, providing protection from sun and wind by wrapping them loosely in cloth that can be removed a layer at a time late in the day.

During this process, plants require frequent watering to keep them from drying out. If an unexpected cold spell arrives, move plants to well-protected areas or cover them. When summer is over and plants return to their winter home, hardening off is less critical, but the transfer should still be done gradually.

SUN AND SHADE

Most houseplants prefer some shade when moved outdoors, but some flowering varieties do well in full sun as long as they are hardened off. Plants' shade preferences vary from full shade to partial shade (a few hours of direct sun) to light or dappled shade (filtered or reflected sun). Check individual entries in the

To harden off or acclimate this palm to the bright sun and outdoor breezes after a winter indoors or even in a greenhouse, cover it with a thin old sheet or sheer curtain for the first day or two, then take the cover off in late afternoon and put it back the next morning, reducing the time of cover each day for 7 to 10 days.

SUN ANGLES

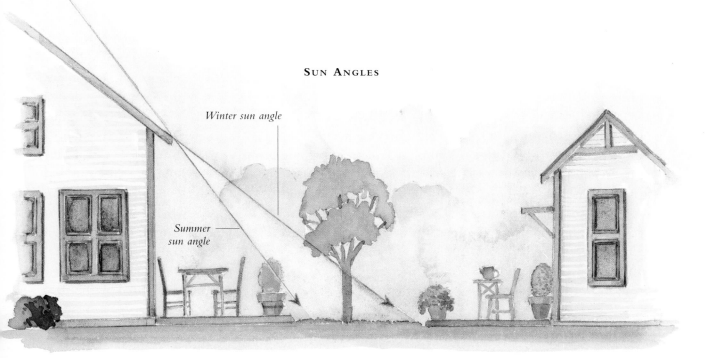

Winter sun angle

Summer sun angle

North ▶

Take note of where structures and trees cast shade during different seasons. Plan terraces and seating areas to maximize comfort year-round.

SUMMER AND WINTER SHADOWS

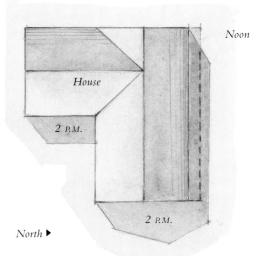

Noon

House

2 P.M.

2 P.M.

North ▶

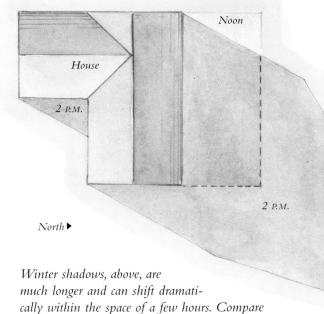

Noon

House

2 P.M.

2 P.M.

North ▶

In summer, only those areas immediately beside the house are shaded. Note how features of the house, such as the roof, affect the shadows below.

Winter shadows, above, are much longer and can shift dramatically within the space of a few hours. Compare the shadow cast at noon with that cast at 2 P.M.

encyclopedia for shade requirements (see page 87).

If you live in an area where you can garden year-round, the angle of the sun, which varies widely from summer to winter, is another consideration. Plants that need full summer sun may not receive enough sun in winter; on the other hand, plants that prefer summer shade, like impatiens, will accept full winter sun. Plants that appreciate full sun in northern states are grateful for more shade, especially afternoon shade, the farther south they grow.

HOW TO PLANT

Deciding whether to create a tropical garden by keeping plants in pots or putting them in the ground depends on a number of factors: where you garden (deck, patio, or yard), climate and length of growing season, types and sizes of plants, and types of containers.

CONTAINERS Keeping plants in pots may be a wise choice if you have problem soil, lack proper sun or shade, or simply don't have room—or time—to plant them in the ground. A shady spot around a tree, for example, is ideal for most houseplants. But under trees like maples, sycamores, and pines, which leach moisture and nutrients from the soil, containers are a good solution.

A plant's growth may be slightly restrained by the size

The glorious mixture of tropical and cold-hardy plants filling these garden containers provides an exotic focal point for the patio. Design: Benjamin H. Hammontree

of its container, but that same restraint often encourages plants to blossom quickly. Tropicals that shoot up rapidly during a long growing season, such as rubber trees, and become too large to dig up, are best grown in pots, as they need to be moved indoors at the first hint of cold weather. When they get too large to trundle back and forth, you can take cuttings or air layers from outdoor plants to overwinter indoors (see page 56), or take

cuttings from indoor plants to move outdoors in spring.

If a plant doesn't thrive soon after its move outdoors, it may be root-bound; if so, repot it in a larger container or divide it. Unless you want to show off a decorative container, burying it in mulch with a few more inches of mulch on top helps retain moisture and reduces watering needs. Sinking a pot directly into the soil also keeps it cool and damp. Put a layer of gravel or plastic over the soil before you put the pot in the ground. This covers the pot's drainage hole and discourages worms and insects you don't want indoors at the end of the season.

IN-GROUND PLANTS Planting a tropical in the ground ensures that it will grow faster with less

Most philodendrons grown as house-plants don't get this big. But if you live in a warm climate, some species will astound you.

care. Digging it up at summer's end, however, is more shocking to the plant than simply moving its container inside.

You can reduce stress by pruning the roots about 3 weeks before an anticipated move. Use a spade or long-bladed knife to cut a circle as wide and deep as the container in which the plant will be potted. Leave the roots that are inside the circle intact and water well. When you cut underneath the plant to lift it into the container, it will have formed new roots. If a plant is simply too large to repot, you can take cuttings and start over again the next year.

Adding New Tropicals

By the time you've enjoyed your houseplants outdoors for one summer, you will probably want to add more. You can buy houseplants to overwinter inside, start seeds in late winter or early spring, or take cuttings from last year's prolific growers. Most trees, shrubs, perennials, and tender tropical plants grown as annuals can be propagated from stem or basal cuttings.

STARTING FROM SEED

Starting from seed is an economical way to get lots of plants. It also allows you to experiment with new and unusual varieties, since most seed catalogs (see page 59) and nursery seed racks offer more choices than you are likely to find among ready-to-plant young plants in pots and cell-packs. You can sow seeds directly outdoors in a planting bed or cutting garden, for example, or in containers for later transplanting to the garden.

STEM OR BASAL CUTTINGS

Stem cuttings, also called "softwood cuttings," are taken from pieces of the stem or shoot. Basal cuttings are quite similar; they consist of entire young shoots, cut from the parent plant so that each retains a piece of firm tissue at its base. Both are rooted in the same way. You can take stem and basal cuttings any time the plant is green, but they root most easily during the active growing season from late spring to early summer.

1 Use clean pots or flats with drainage holes. Fill them with sterile medium (such as vermiculite, perlite, a mixture of perlite and peat moss, or potting soil). Dampen the mixture and pat it down firmly.

2 Take cuttings early in the day, when plants are full of moisture. Look for a plant that is healthy and growing vigorously. With a sharp knife or bypass pruners, snip 5- to 6-inch-long pieces from the plant, choosing a vigorous young tip or side shoots.

Remove and discard any flower buds, flowers, and small shoots growing laterally from the main stem. Trim the stems into 3- to 4-inch lengths, each with at least two nodes (growing points). Make the lower cut just below a node, since new roots will form at this point. Remove leaves from the lower half of the cutting.

For plants with very large leaves, use scissors to cut away most of the large leaves, leaving only a small area of leaf. Do not cut away small new leaves emerging from the stem end.

Air Layering

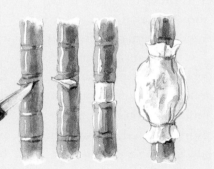

Air layering is most successful if done while a plant is growing actively. To encourage such growth in houseplants, fertilize the plant to be layered, then place it in a sunny window. When new leaves appear, proceed with layering.

Begin below a node. Make a slanting cut (insert a wooden matchstick to keep it open) in the bark or remove a ring of bark. Dust the cut with rooting hormone, encase it in damp sphagnum moss, and then cover with plastic wrap to keep the moss moist.

If layering succeeds, roots will appear in the moss after a few months; you can then sever the rooted stem from the parent and pot it. At this point, it's usually a good idea to remove about half the new plant's leaves to prevent excessive moisture loss through transpiration while it gets established.

If no roots form, the cut you made will form a callus, and new bark will eventually grow over it.

3 Dip the lower cut ends of the cuttings in liquid or powdered rooting hormone; shake off any excess. (Many gardeners omit this step.)

Using the end of a pencil, make 1- to 1½-inch-deep holes in the rooting medium, spacing them 1 to 2 inches apart; then insert the cuttings. Firm the medium around the cuttings and water with a fine spray. Label each container with the plant name and the date.

Enclose each container in a plastic bag. Close the bag to maintain humidity, but open it for a few minutes every day to provide ventilation. Set the containers in a warm, shaded (but not dark) location.

4 The cuttings will usually take hold and begin growing roots in 1 to 5 weeks. Keep the medium moist but not soggy. To check, gently pull on a cutting; if you feel resistance, roots are forming. At this point, expose the cuttings to drier air by opening the bags. If the cuttings wilt, close the bags again for a few days (opening them briefly each day).

When the plants seem acclimated to open air, transplant each to its own 3- to 4-inch pot of lightweight potting mix. When they're well rooted and growing new leaves, they're ready to go into the ground or into containers.

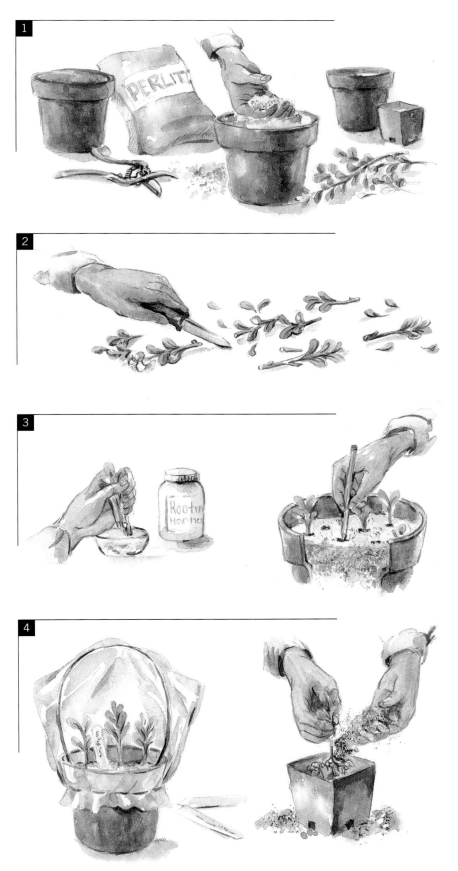

Traveling with Seeds, Cuttings, and Plants

Bringing home tropical plants from another state is not usually a problem, but it can be complicated—if not impossible—to bring home tropical plants from other countries because of agricultural inspections and quarantines. Seeds, however, are usually not a problem. Just keep them dry and away from extreme heat. Freezing won't hurt them and is actually a good way to keep them for long periods. Before popping seeds into the freezer, label them with name, color, plant size, and any other information you might forget before planting.

Collect tropical cuttings close to travel time. Choose cuttings from healthy, well-watered plants; soak stem ends in water for up to 24 hours before packing in plastic bags with some wet vermiculite or perlite. Leave bag tops open, and keep bags in bright light (not direct sunlight) until you are ready to go. Close bags and tuck them into carry-on luggage for plane travel.

To check potted plants through on a plane, pack the pots in a box filled with loose packing material; seal the top as late as possible. If you drive, leave the bags slightly open so that the plants can absorb any humidity.

If you relocate, most movers will carry plants but refuse to be responsible for them. Plants should survive as long as they don't freeze.

EXPERIMENTING WITH TROPICALS

The only limits to experimenting with new plants involve your time, energy, and pocketbook. Most gardeners find time and money spent on plants both satisfying and rewarding. Universities and botanical gardens that experiment with new tropical species, like Miami University, in Oxford, Ohio, and Boerner Botanical Gardens, near Milwaukee, Wisconsin, are good places to visit; they often have plant sales with unusual varieties.

Acquiring seeds and cuttings from other people is often the way friendships are born. Most people are happy that you

ABOVE: *Bromeliads and variegated shell ginger* (Alpinia zerumbet) *epitomize the tropics.* BELOW: *A collection of succulents blends with annuals and pink calla lilies* (Zantedeschia rehmanii). *Design: DeWayne Gallatin/Calloway Gardens*

noticed a plant, will give details about its growth habits, and often volunteer cuttings, seedlings, divisions, or seeds.

Tropical Specialty Nurseries

Most nurseries, garden centers, and catalogs have some tropical plants, but they may be in the greenhouse or houseplant section. When you have exhausted those sources, here are some specialty nurseries that have both excellent selections and a great deal of information—and often photos—of various cultivars. Choosing nurseries close to your area usually results in a better selection of plants and information appropriate to your climate. If you don't find what you're looking for, widen your search.

A few nurseries offer seeds of tropical plants, an inexpensive means of expanding your stock and adding excitement to your winter windowsills. The encyclopedia will tell you which tropical plants grow quickly from seeds (see page 87); vines are good bets.

ALOHA TROPICALS
1247 Browning Court
Vista, CA 92083
(760) 941-0920
www.alohatropicals.com
By appointment only
Plants, bulbs

THE BAMBOO GARDEN
1507 SE Alder Street
Portland, OR 97214
(503) 654-0024
www.bamboogarden.com
Large selection of bamboo

THE BANANA TREE, INC.
715 Northampton Street
Easton, PA 18042
(610) 253-9589
www.banana-tree.com
Seeds, rhizomes, tubers

BRENT AND BECKY'S BULBS
7900 Daffodil Lane
Gloucester, VA 23061
(804) 693-3966
www.brentandbeckysbulbs.com
Hardy and tender bulbs

COMPANION PLANTS
7247 N. Coolville Ridge Road
Athens, OH 45701
(740) 592-4643
www.frognet.net/companion_plants/
Seeds, plants

THE EXOTIC PLUMERIA
Offices: 500 Highland Avenue
Nursery: 453 MLK Blvd. West
Seffner, FL 33584-5016
(813) 653-2496
www.exoticplumeria.com
Large selection of plumerias

GLASSHOUSE WORKS
Church Street
P.O. Box 97
Stewart, OH 45778-0097
(740) 662-2142
www.glasshouseworks.com
Plants

J. L. HUDSON, SEEDSMAN
Star Route 2, Box 337
La Honda, CA 94020
www.jlhudsonseeds.net
Seeds

LILYPONS WATER GARDENS
6800 Lilypons Road
P.O. Box 10
Buckeystown, MD 21717-0010
(800) 999-5459
www.lilypons.com
Water plants

LOGEE'S GREENHOUSES
141 North Street
Danielson, CT 06239
(888) 330-8038
www.logees.com
Plants

PARK SEED COMPANY
1 Parkton Avenue
Greenwood, SC 29647
(800) 213-0076
www.parkseed.com
Plants, seeds

PLANT DELIGHTS NURSERY
9241 Sauls Road
Raleigh, NC 27603
(919) 772-4794
www.plantdelights.com
Plants

SINGING SPRINGS NURSERY
8802 Wilkerson Road
Cedar Grove, NC 27231
(919) 732-9403
www.singingspringsnursery.com
Uncommon plants

STOKES TROPICALS
4806 E. Old Spanish Trail
Jeanerette, LA 70544
(337) 365-6998
www.stokestropicals.com
Plants

TROPIFLORA
3530 Tallevast Road
Sarasota, FL 34243
(941) 351-2267
www.tropiflora.com
Plants

YUCCADO NURSERY
P.O. Box 907
Hempstead, TX 77445
(979) 826-4580
www.yuccado.com
Drought- and heat-resistant plants

CHAPTER FOUR

Tropicals Under Cover

AFTER SPENDING A SIZZLING SUMMER OUTSIDE, some tropicals can retreat indoors to fill windowsills and vacant corners of your home for the fall, winter, and early spring months. Placing a tall palm or a banana in a corner by a sunny window and adding other tropical plants simply transforms the whole room. Not only do exotics decorate a room, but they also provide you with familiar, more mature plants for the next year's garden. ∾ Sunrooms and garden rooms are perfect places for both people and plants. Greenhouses are more functional, with benches of plants at a handy working height under hanging plants overhead. Either environment allows your treasured tropicals to spend the cold months in comfort, emerging in late spring to make an immediate impact on your garden.

Window Gardens

Bringing plants indoors preserves more than your best stock; it reminds you of summer's success and inspires you with even more lavish garden plans for the next year.

Considering the differences between a dry, heated house and a humid, tropical jungle, it's amazing that so many exotic plants are adaptable to changing environments. To ensure success in moving plants indoors, make a list in late summer of the stars of your tropical garden and check the plant encyclopedia (page 87) for the best winter conditions. For those that will become houseplants, check their light requirements before deciding where to put them. You can allow maximum access to light by layering containers, with smaller ones in front or on top of larger ones; placing trailing plants where they can cascade over shelves; or hanging plants from hooks.

TOP RIGHT: *A collection of houseplants warms a winter room.* BELOW: *Cyclamen, Jerusalem cherry* (Solanum pseudocapsicum), *and Christmas cactus* (Schlumbergera × buckleyi) *add colorful touches. Design: Little & Lewis Inc.*

MOVING INDOORS

While plants are still outdoors, prune them as needed, including tops and roots of the large plants you want to dig up (see page 55). Two weeks before the move, decrease water to toughen plant tissues. Consider individual plant needs; some need more protection from cool weather than others. All tropicals except the ones you will dig up as bulbs must go inside before a frost; roots and tubers should go into a basement or other dark place a few days later.

Gradual reintroduction is not as crucial when a plant is moving inside, but plants will benefit by being moved first to a protected porch or patio. Here they can still enjoy outdoor humidity, acclimatize somewhat to lower temperatures and light levels, and be at hand in case a sudden cold wave prompts a quick indoor move.

ABOVE: *Long-blooming moth orchids* (Phalaenopsis) *add elegance to a sunny space.* RIGHT: *Yellow shrimp plant* (Pachystachys lutea), *dracaena, and other tropicals winter indoors.*

PROVIDING THE RIGHT HOME

It's harder to grow any plant indoors in winter than it is to grow plants outdoors in summer; the longer the winter, the more difficult it is. Though not all your plants may thrive, the successes are well worth the challenge. Providing the best possible growing conditions for the plant is the best way to ensure a good result.

PROTECTION FROM COLD Any
plant too near a window on a cold night will freeze, so make sure that plants don't touch the glass. If severe cold is expected, insert a piece of heavy opaque paper between the plant and the window at night, and remove it in the morning. Some plants are even susceptible to hot and cold drafts in the house; keep them away from exterior doorways and heating vents.

In their natural environment, tropicals are accustomed to temperatures that are warm in the daytime and cooler at night (but no lower than 60°F/16°C). Turning the thermostat down as much as 10 degrees at night helps both plants and budget.

LIGHT LEVELS Light is the most
important aspect of plant culture. Some plants are happiest in south-facing windows or in bay windows that capture the sun. North-facing windows are suitable for shade-loving tropicals. Occasionally check on the

plants; if a plant seems to be doing well, don't move it. But if a plant starts to droop, develop strange spots, drop more than a few leaves (all plants lose some leaves when moved), or appear otherwise unhappy, move it somewhere else until you notice a marked improvement.

Bromeliads are easy houseguests; just keep water in their whorls. Pink Aechmea *offers color for months, as do* Guzmania *and* Neoregelia.

WATERING Overwatering is the biggest killer of indoor plants. Because plants grow more slowly in winter, they need less water. Check plants every day or two to make sure the soil is damp. Pay particular attention to plants that have been moved indoors recently, hanging plants, and plants in small containers. Plants with large leaves and a large root mass need more water than smaller, younger plants.

If a plant's soil feels dry, add water until it starts to run out the drainage hole into the saucer.

Using watering cans with long, curving spouts and planting in hanging containers that can be raised and lowered make the job easier. Avoid containers without a drainage hole; only gardenias and a few aquatic plants, such as *Cyperus,* can survive standing constantly in water. For other plants, allow the water to sit in the saucer for about 20 minutes before emptying it.

If light conditions allow, simplify watering by grouping plants that need a lot of water or other attention. For instance, bromeliads like to have water sitting in their "vases," or whorls, but prefer the soil to be fairly dry. And different varieties of orchids have different water needs because of their fast-draining organic planting medium.

HUMIDITY Lack of humidity can eventually kill tropicals that are wintering indoors after a moist summer outside. So acclimate plants by bringing them indoors before you turn on your furnace.

Though it's difficult to duplicate the moisture that tropical plants are accustomed to in their natural environment, you can raise humidity levels inside. Grouping plants provides some comfort, and setting containers on trays of gravel or stone chips with water added just below the bottoms of the pots will increase humidity as the water evaporates. Adding a humidifier benefits both plants and people.

Even misting plants with a sprayer several times a day is helpful. Buy plastic spray bottles at any nursery or garden store, or recycle any bottle that formerly contained a nontoxic household product. Mist early in the day so that the foliage is dry by nightfall. Avoid spraying orchids in bright sunlight; some orchids develop spots on their leaves. If you have sufficient light and space, move tropical plants to naturally humid areas: in bathrooms and laundry rooms, and near kitchen sinks.

SOIL AND CONTAINERS Though soil in the tropics varies from sand to clay, it's always rich in humus made up of plant and animal matter. Water doesn't stand on top of the soil but drains through, and the soil never dries out completely. Because soil doesn't pack down around plants, it provides plenty of air around their roots.

When repotting a tropical, always use a clean pot with good drainage. If you want to use a decorative container without a drainage hole, place a smaller pot inside. Fill the smaller pot with soil, up to about an inch below the pot rim. After watering the plant, empty the outer container so that no water stands around the plant's roots.

The type of mix you use depends on how long the plant is going to be in the container. For short-term use, mix half soil and half sphagnum peat moss; for long-term use (more than 9 months), mix soil with coarser matter such as fine bark chips or calcined clay. These components decompose more slowly than peat moss, helping to keep sufficient oxygen in the soil.

Buy sterilized soil or soil mix to ensure that your soil is free of insect eggs, soil-borne pathogens, and weed seeds. When buying soil mix, read the list of ingredients and add coarse matter if needed. Make a mixture of one-third soil, one-third coarse matter, and one-third humus.

Most orchids and epiphytic plants don't grow in soil but rather in clumps of organic matter. You can buy special orchid mix in nurseries and garden

No-Soil Potting Mixes

If you need a large volume of potting mix, you may be able to save money by making your own. The basic mix is made with nitrogen-free fertilizer, so it can be stored up to a year. (Nitrogen dissipates more quickly than the potassium and phosphorus used in this mix.) If you plant during the growing season, use a complete fertilizer about 2 weeks after planting.

Basic No-Soil Mix
You can use this for all but acid-loving plants. These amounts will make a little more than 1 cubic yard (9 cubic feet) of mix.

2/3 cubic yard nitrogen-stabilized bark or Canadian sphagnum peat moss

1/3 cubic yard washed 20-grit sand

6 pounds 0-10-10 dry fertilizer

10 pounds dolomite or dolomite limestone

Acid No-Soil Mix
Use this mix for tropical rhododendrons, camellias, heather *(Calluna vulgaris)*, most ferns, and other acid-loving plants.

4 to 5 parts coarse peat moss

1 part leaf mold

Poinsettias (Euphorbia pulcherrima), *amaryllis* (Hippeastrum), *ivy* (Hedera), *and philodendron* (Philodendron bipinnatifidum) *brighten the winter season.*

Customizing Commercial Mixes

You can tailor potting mixes for special container needs.

Extra-Lightweight Mix

Use this for hanging baskets or other locations where weight is a consideration. It dries out quickly—be sure to monitor watering needs.

2 parts commercial potting mix or Basic No-Soil Mix (page 65)

1 part perlite or vermiculite

Rich Mix

Plants grown for their foliage may benefit from extra-rich potting soil. Add timed-release fertilizer to the mix, according to package directions, when you plant.

2 parts commercial potting mix

1 part well-composted chicken manure

1 part redwood soil conditioner

Wandering Jew (Tradescantia fluminensis) *in a hanging basket thrives in an extra-lightweight no-soil mix.*

stores or from an orchid-supply catalog. Special plant mixes are also available for other types of plants, such as the sandy soils preferred by cacti and succulents, and a quick-draining bromeliad soil mixture that includes sand, rice hulls, or white rocks. Mixes containing little soil are especially suitable for large pots because they don't make pots too heavy to move easily.

FEEDING PLANTS Plants that grow slowly through the winter need little fertilizer. After moving them indoors, don't feed until they show signs of new growth. This may not happen until the days lengthen toward spring. When you start fertilizing, keep the following suggestions in mind for best results:

- Water a plant thoroughly at least several hours before applying fertilizer.
- Don't feed a plant suffering from pests or disease; wait until it recovers before encouraging it to grow.
- Don't overfertilize. Read labels and use less rather than more. Some growers recommend using fertilizers at half strength and feeding twice as often to provide the plant with nutrients at a continuous rate; others suggest applying fertilizers in light doses with each watering.
- Use a fertilizer recommended specifically for houseplant foliage and blooms.

PESTS AND DISEASES The best way to avoid pests and diseases is to maintain healthy growing conditions. If plants are robust and healthy, they'll be more disease-resistant and less likely to attract pests. Make sure that plants coming inside to spend the winter are pest-free before they enter. Treat them to a good shower and an application of soapy water before bringing them indoors, and continue to check carefully for pests for several weeks.

If you discover disease or pests, treat immediately and isolate affected plants for a couple of weeks so that problems don't spread. Most gardeners today opt for natural and mechanical pest controls instead of chemical insecticides. These include hosing off small insects such as aphids, washing plants with nontoxic soaps, and hand-picking pests such as slugs and snails (deposit in soapy water to kill them). You can make your own nontoxic soap spray by adding a teaspoon each of dishwashing liquid and cooking oil to ½ quart of water. If plants spend the winter in a greenhouse, introduce biological controls such as lacewings to eat plant-destroying insects.

Pests target stressed plants. As winter progresses, plant stress is usually due to lack of humidity. Moving the plant to a shower or tub for an occasional soaping and soaking will help.

GARDENING WITH ARTIFICIAL LIGHT

When natural light is insufficient for plants, you can add artificial light in the form of spotlights, fluorescent tubes, or grow lights. Incandescent lights help flowering and growth, but they can burn foliage if placed closer than 2 feet from the plant.

Cool-white fluorescent bulbs produce compact foliage. Place them as close as 4 to 6 inches above the plants and no farther away than 18 to 24 inches; keep bulbs clean and change them once a year. Grow lights are good but expensive. Spotlights produce both heat and light for spectacular effect. Use overlapping flood-

Peace lily (Spathiphyllum wallisii), *lady palm* (Rhapis), *and Chinese evergreen* (Aglaonema modestum) *do well in low light.*

lights to increase light levels for a grouping of large plants, and concentrated spots for one plant.

Leave any light on for 10 to 18 hours a day (a timer is handy), and darken the room at night.

Sunrooms and Greenhouses

When you run out of room indoors for a winter tropical garden, consider a bay window on the south-facing wall or better yet, a sunroom with plenty of glass and heat (60°F/16°C at night) to keep plants healthy. A small greenhouse will preserve even more plants. Improvements in glazing materials and structural design have led to more choices than ever before.

SUNROOMS

An indoor garden room, solarium, or conservatory is designed for the comfort of both plants and people. If this sunny space adjoins a kitchen or living room, it will quickly become a natural place for the overflow of family and guests. If it's located at a front entrance, the area acts as a buffer between outside and interior climates; as a back entrance it becomes a natural mudroom—a perfect place to shed coats and garden shoes while enjoying flowers and fragrances.

You'll find books with a wealth of design information on adding or adapting sunny spaces for plants and people. A sunroom can be built from stock windows, doors, and skylights; custom-made; or purchased in modular kit form. When planning for a sunroom or other indoor garden room, consider the basic needs of both plants and people: a floor that withstands dampness, win- dows that open for ventilation, perhaps a skylight, and space for seating.

CLIMATE CONTROL Because a sunroom is part of the home, ventilation, heating, and climate control are usually extensions of the house's heating and cooling systems. Your aim is to duplicate the natural environment of your tropical plants. Obviously some spots in the room will be warmer than others, so arrange your plants with this in mind. Some plants like it hot; others can be cool.

Succulents, begonias, ferns, and brightly colored tropical foliage surround a chaise longue.

WATER ACCESS Your home's plumbing system also may have to be extended to provide plants with water. Whether or not you need a connection depends on how many plants spend the winter indoors and how far the area is from a water source.

SUNSHADES AND FILTERS To reduce heat gain on warm days and prevent heat loss in cloudy, damp weather, consider installing awnings to shade the sunroom windows. Some can be retracted from the inside; others, sensing the sun and wind, open and close automatically.

Draperies, vertical blinds, or roll-up, Roman, or pleated shades make soft screens. Exterior solar screens of woven fiberglass mesh pull up or down as needed to filter and soften summer sun while allowing breezes to enter.

GREENHOUSES

Many gardeners harbor a secret wish for a small greenhouse that will preserve their plants—and mental health—through long winter months and allow them to propagate new plants easily. A new interest in gardening under cover has led to a

ABOVE LEFT: *A variety of foliage fills a sunroom.* ABOVE RIGHT: *Orchids add opulence.* LEFT: *In warm contrast to the snowy scene outside, potted palms and rattan convey a sense of tropical warmth. Architect: Rob Whitten*

broader range of greenhouse choices than ever before.

A greenhouse differs from a sunroom or conservatory in that it is more functional than decorative, designed for plants rather than people. It can be attached to the house—a most pleasant choice in cold-winter climates—or freestanding. And greenhouses filled with tropical plants, most of which move outdoors in the summer, may become protected picnic sites.

VENTILATION Ventilation is important for maintaining a constant temperature in sunrooms or greenhouses. It also provides good air circulation and keeps humidity and carbon dioxide at optimum levels. Louvered or hinged intake vents placed low on greenhouse walls allow cool air to enter. Because warm air rises, roof or ridge vents are helpful. Roof vents should be about 15 percent larger than intake vents. Place them on the side of the roof away from prevailing summer winds. An exhaust fan system is an alternative to roof vents.

Vents can be opened and closed manually or automatically; all vents should be able to be closed tightly. When they're opened, screening keeps out pests. Make sure the screening is not so fine that it interferes with the airflow.

Venting from the house into an attached greenhouse or sunroom through interior windows or doors can provide fresh air and help regulate warmth to both buildings.

SHADING AND CLIMATE CONTROL Shading in hotter, brighter months is necessary to control overheating and to protect the plants still inside from sunburn. Shade cloths inside or whitewash covering the outside of the glass will do the job.

Fortunately, much of a greenhouse can now be operated auto-

A connected greenhouse easily ties in to a home's utility lines.

matically. Fans and vents can be thermostatically controlled, with vents either motorized or opened by heat-activated pistons. Timers and humidistats can activate irrigation, misting, and fogging systems. You can install controls for these functions in the greenhouse or integrate them into a computerized climate controller that you manipulate on-site or from a remote computer.

Greenhouse in Disguise

Gardeners who live in areas where deed restrictions prohibit greenhouses have found creative alternatives. One Florida gardener designed and built a beautiful arbor just outside a screened-in pool area for her 400 orchid plants. Side panels of white lath enclose shelves and benches, and a cloth shade covers a fiberglass ceiling that helps to provide a pleasant environment for her plants.

The air circulation through the arbor's lath is wonderful in summer; for winter protection, the rolls of plastic that hide along the top inside framing of the arbor during most of the year can be rolled down to completely enclose the area. A butane heater keeps the temperature at 60°F/16°C even on the coldest nights.

ALARM SYSTEMS A temperature alarm can save plants if your heating system fails. Some alarm systems are battery-operated; others operate on home current and should have a battery backup. Some even automatically telephone a service bureau to alert it about a problem. Most home security systems can incorporate a greenhouse temperature alarm. Install the alarm sensor in a shady, dry place in the greenhouse, and locate the ringer or buzzer where you are most likely to hear it in the dead of a cold night.

Sunset's *Greenhouses* book also has plans and instructions for choosing, building, and using greenhouses and sunrooms. If you're looking for a greenhouse, mail-order and custom-made models are available. Until you acquire your own, you might choose to rent greenhouse space for your plants in the winter.

WATERING BASICS

Watering with a hose makes plant care much easier. You can wash dust and disease organisms off of foliage, keep plants well misted, and water plants according to individual needs. Fill containers with enough water to reach the pot rim. Set the nozzle so that the force of the water provides a gentle irrigation. Keep hose nozzles and ends off the floor to avoid transferring bacteria or disease organisms from them to plants.

Greenhouses often utilize low-volume overhead sprinklers to save on water and allow better control of spray patterns. Most

Cymbidium *orchids and ivy are placed on a sunroom floor to make watering and other winter care easier.*

gardeners, however, prefer watering by hand according to the plants' needs.

Drip irrigation is another alternative. A drip system delivers small amounts of water to individual containers through a network of thin tubes and emitters; you customize the layout according to your needs. Water is delivered slowly, soaking each plant's root area with little loss of water to evaporation or runoff. Two advantages of this system are that the foliage stays dry and the plants receive a constant supply of water. Installing an automatic timer ensures that plants are well watered when you are away.

This detached greenhouse, covered with vines that offer shade in summer, is a garden focal point, charming both inside and out.

CHAPTER FIVE

Growing for Success

UNLESS YOU ARE GARDENING IN THE WARMEST and wettest of climate zones, your tropicals are going to need good basic care to attain the greatest growth in a single season. When they get off to a good start in early spring, they require no more work than other plants to make a major impact in your garden. The rewards justify the labor of carrying plants inside and out, or covering and uncovering them, as weather dictates. With plenty of water and the right amount of fertilizer, these fantastic plants will thrive and bloom. ∾ After months of enjoyment comes the challenge of protecting plants through the cold months. It may be easier to discard poor performers and small, easily available plants at the end of the growing season; larger and more expensive specimens should be saved. You'll find out how to keep plants protected so that your garden becomes a showplace every summer.

A Spring Start

Even after a warm winter, tropicals need tender loving care. So keep them out of the spotlight, shifting attention to more minor performers, until they recover their beauty. When warm weather returns, a good spring pruning to remove dead foliage gives the desired face-lift.

SPRING PRUNING

Pruning dead foliage should wait until after the final frost; even dry, brown leaves offer plants protection when temperatures dip. Keep a plant's growth habits in mind as you prune: plants that look dead can come back from their roots or even from top growth. When no green growth is evident, start pruning fairly high on the stem, cutting back until you find signs of life.

Remove dead foliage and broken or crowded branches. The wood's flexibility is an indicator of whether that section is alive; pencil-size dead branches tend to break off easily. If you have pruned all the way back to new root shoots, remove all but one for a tree; leave several for a shrub.

SPRING PLANTING

Unless you put all your tropicals in containers, planting starts with good garden soil.

It's important to know how the soil drains. While some tropicals thrive in perpetually moist areas, most require well-drained soil. You can improve drainage by adding organic matter, but if drainage is extremely slow, you might consider planting in another part of the garden or keeping plants in containers.

SOIL TESTING Soils may be acid, neutral, or alkaline. Alkaline soils are usually found in dry-summer regions with low rainfall, while acid types are associated with high rainfall and humid summers. Most tropicals prefer a slightly acid medium, so you might want to test your soil. Kits sold in nurseries and garden centers will give you a ballpark reading. For more precise information, send a soil sample to a laboratory (look in the yellow pages under "Laboratories—Analytical") or check with your Cooperative Extension Office. It may be easier to keep sensitive plants in containers.

Careful attention in spring ensures sumptuous summer success for tropicals in containers or in the ground.
Design: Lisa Ray

A well-prepared border of red salvias and dahlias blooms early and constantly against the green of ginger foliage.

Caladiums and impatiens can stay in the ground in frost-free climates and go back outside in spring elsewhere.

PREPARING A PLANTING BED If you're planting in an existing bed, all you'll need to do is add soil amendments in and around each new planting hole. But if you are planting in a new area, you'll need to put some time and effort into preparation. Begin by removing sod and controlling weeds; then loosen the soil and work in amendments.

Planting preparation can begin as late as spring if the soil is not too damp. To test the soil, mold a handful into a ball. If it crumbles easily when dropped, it's dry enough to work; if not, wait a while. Don't try to dig in soil that is too wet or completely dry.

Use a sharp spade to cut sod into sections, and then push the spade under each section to sever the roots. Lift the sections away with your hands. (See the illustration at top right.)

In small areas you can use a spade to loosen soil; for larger beds you may wish to use a rotary tiller. Dig to a depth of 10 to 12 inches, breaking up clods of earth and removing stones as you go.

The next step is to amend the soil with organic matter, fertilizer, and any materials needed to correct the pH, as shown (see the bottom illustration). Organic matter improves both clay and sand—and it helps plants grow even better in loam. Organic materials include compost (homemade or purchased), wood byproducts fortified with nitrogen (such as ground bark and sawdust), aged manure, and peat moss; other choices may be available locally.

Use generous quantities of organic matter, spreading a layer at least 3 to 4 inches thick over the loosened soil. (Aged manure is an exception; too much can burn roots and leach excess nutrients into the groundwater. To be on the safe side, spread it in a layer just 1 inch thick.) As a rule of thumb, a cubic yard of organic material should cover 100 square feet of planting to a depth of 3 inches. Also add any amendments needed to alter soil pH at this time.

With a spading fork or tiller, incorporate all the amendments into the soil. Then level the bed with a rake and water well. If possible, let the soil settle for a few weeks before setting out plants. When you do plant, the soil will be easy to work, and planting will be a pleasure.

PLANTING IN THE GROUND When the weather is warm enough (55–60°F/13–16°C at night), set out plants, spacing them far enough apart to prevent crowding. Starting with the largest, most dramatic plant, shuffle your plants around until you have a satisfactory arrangement. Plants that remain in containers can be rearranged easily later.

Soak the plant, still in its pot, in a bucket of water for about 30 minutes or until the soil is completely dampened.

Dig a hole, making it the same depth as the container and an inch or two wider (see below). Remove the pot.

With your fingers, gently separate matted roots. If there's a pad of coiled white roots at the pot bottom, cut or pull it off so that new roots will form and grow into the soil. Place each plant in its hole so that the top of the root ball is even with the soil surface. If the roots have pushed up above the level of the soil in the pot, as potted palms often do, sink the ball low enough that the crown is just at soil level and all the roots are covered. You can amend the soil in each hole to suit individual needs. For instance, plants such as elephant's ear *(Colocasia esculenta)* and bird of paradise *(Strelitzia reginae)* like damp soil, so you can add a water-absorbing gel to the lower soil layers to retain moisture.

Firm soil around the roots. Water large plants well before you add the last layer of soil, and make a depression in the soil around the outer rim of foliage to catch and hold water. Spread a thin layer of mulch to keep the soil cool, conserve moisture, and discourage weeds. To lessen the possibility of rot, keep the mulch an inch or two away from each plant's crown. Water diligently until plants are established; then water less often and more deeply.

PLANTING BARE-ROOT TROPICALS
Most tropical plants now come from nurseries in pots. Any that arrive bare-root (with soil removed from the roots) have lighter organic matter packed around the roots and are enclosed in plastic. If you dig up your own plants, leave as much soil as possible on the roots, keep plants moist, and reset quickly.

If you'll be setting out plants in a day or two, put them in a bucket, add a little water, and store in a cool place. If planting must be delayed for more than a few days, pot up the plants in small containers or heel them in—plant them temporarily in a shallow trench in the garden.

Before setting out plants in permanent positions, prepare a planting bed. If you are adding plants to an existing bed, work a shovelful of organic material into the soil around each new plant.

Remove the packing material and soak the roots in water for about 30 minutes. Dig a hole about twice as wide as the root system (see above). Then make a cone of soil in the center to support the roots. Set the plant on top of the cone and spread the roots evenly. Fill the hole with soil so that the plant's crown is level with or slightly

A container of tropicals comes together quickly, looks good from the first day on, and lasts indefinitely if you winter it indoors. Design: Tina Dixon

above the soil, and water well. Finally, spread a thin layer of mulch around the plant.

PLANTING IN CONTAINERS For a lush look, fill large pots with tropical (and tropical-looking) plants. Start with a pot at least 24 inches in diameter and 17 to 20 inches deep. Using a drill with a ½-inch glass-and-tile bit, drill three or four additional drainage holes around the drain hole in the bottom of the pot.

Fill the pot with premium planting mix to about 6 inches below the rim. Add water and blend it to completely moisten the mix. Tamp the soil down slightly.

Arrange plants in their nursery containers atop the soil. Remove the tallest plant from its nursery container, rough up its root ball, and plant it.

Repeat the process with lower-growing plants; place trailers around the edge. Add soil to raise the level to 1 to 2 inches below the rim. Scatter slow-release fertilizer over the soil, and water.

Hard-Pruning for Cold Climates

Large-leafed, cold-hardy trees can contribute to an exotic setting when used as a backdrop or frame for your tropical garden. If you start with a tree that's only a few years old and cut it back to within 6 inches of ground level in late winter or early spring, tender shoots rising from the trunk will quickly grow into straight stems with very large leaves. Make cuts just above a bud or pair of buds.

Hard-pruning works especially well on the trees listed below. It yields even more effective results if you choose cultivars with colorful leaves. Flowering trees cut back in this way can grow up to 15 feet tall in a growing season. They usually don't bloom, but the foliage effect is what is important.

Empress tree *(Paulownia tomentosa)*
Golden catalpa *(Catalpa bignonioides* 'Aurea')
Golden elderberry *(Sambucus canadensis* 'Aurea')
Purple smoke tree *(Cotinus coggygria* 'Royal Purple')

Summer Maintenance

To give tropical plants their best chances for luxuriant growth and abundant bloom, it's important to establish good patterns of watering, feeding, mulching, weeding, pruning, and protection from pests and diseases. Removing dead flowers and spent annuals will keep your garden in photo-perfect condition.

WATERING

Tropical plants need a large amount of water—about an inch a week, and more in very hot or windy weather. What Mother Nature doesn't supply, a hose must. A rain gauge gives an accurate measure of rainfall and helps prevent overwatering, which also can be detrimental to plants.

Soaker hoses not only save water but are also very efficient for watering plant roots. Most designs allow 100 feet/30.5 meters of hose for each water outlet, enough for a small garden. If your garden is larger, you can lay separate soaker hoses in various parts of the yard and connect them on a rotating basis.

Two inexpensive methods can be used to water the root balls of large new plants. Fill a 5-gallon bucket that has a small hole in the bottom and set it near the plant; the water will slowly percolate deep into the soil. Or make perforations along a length of plastic drainpipe or a large tin can and place it in the planting hole next to the root ball. Lay one end as deep as the root ball, extending the other end above the soil to the top of the mulch layer. As you water, fill up the pipe or can. Where soil freezes in winter, you can use the pipe to conduct tepid water to a plant's roots. Fill the pipe with mulch, coarse gravel, or insulation material.

Even if you use water-wise methods, remember that most tropicals like rain, so apply short but frequent overhead sprinklings, too. Water early in the morning or early enough in the late afternoon to ensure that foliage dries out by nightfall.

FEEDING

You don't need to add fertilizer at planting time, but if you do, use only a slight amount to keep from stressing roots. Two weeks after planting, water with a liquid fertilizer at half strength. Use a fertilizer that has equal levels of nitrogen, phosphorus, and potassium, as well as trace elements. Once flowering plants are big enough to bloom, you can use a bloom-booster fertilizer with lower levels of nitrogen. Don't overfertilize, though, or you will burn the plants, and don't fertilize after August, or you'll encourage new growth too late in the season or keep plants from going dormant.

MULCHING

Mulch is the best thing you can give to any plant in any garden. It absorbs moisture and nutrients, keeping them from evaporating and the soil from drying out and cracking. It also keeps soil cool around plant roots. As organic mulch breaks down, it continually enriches and improves any soil, encouraging earthworms and beneficial microbes. The warmer the weather, the quicker the mulch breaks down, so replenish it during the season. Keep a 2- to 3-inch layer on the ground, pulling it back several inches from the plant trunk or crown.

Mulch deters weeds and makes them easier to pull. Remove weeds with roots intact before they produce seed; toss them on a compost pile to decompose. By August, tropicals will probably crowd out or shade out most of the weeds.

Though early weeding is important, by August tropicals crowd out weeds.

SUMMER PRUNING

Pruning keeps plants from crowding too closely together. Proper pruning allows them room to spread and ensures that they have plenty of air. Keep pruners handy whenever you walk into the garden, as tropical growth is rapid and shaping is essential.

While you shape, keep the plant's growth pattern in mind. When you pinch or prune the tops off of most plants, side shoots develop and the plants become compact and bushy. For plants like angel's trumpet *(Brugmansia)* that need a wide canopy for a floral umbrella, you may want to remove some low branches to emphasize the fountain formation.

If you pinch the tips of plants that send up shoots from their roots, such as true ginger *(Zingiber officinale)* or lobster-claw *(Heliconia),* no side branching occurs, and the stem eventually withers back to the root. Wait to prune this type of plant until it flowers, or shorten a long shoot only if it's in the way. Staking is an alternative, though it's seldom needed in a tropical garden.

Never cut the top center bud out of a palm—that's where it grows; just remove lower fronds as they die back. One tip: cutting fronds while they are still partly green is easier than waiting until they turn brown.

Pruning can affect bloom. Plants that bloom on old wood, such as Brazilian plume flower

Hardy windmill palm (Trachycarpus fortunei) *needs lower branches pruned as they fade, and removing blooms from caladiums keeps foliage flourishing, but begonias, ivy* (Hedera), *and elephant's ear* (Colocasia esculenta) *need pruning only to remove any dead foliage. Design: Bill Dement and Ed Sessoms*

(Justicia carnea), should be pruned only once a year, shortly after they bloom. But plants that bloom on new wood, like golden wonder senna *(Senna splendida),* can be pruned any time—and pruning will encourage plants like bougainvillea to produce flowers instead of foliage.

You can change woody plants from shrubs to trees or trees to shrubs. But if you change a plant's natural growth pattern too dramatically, the amount of pruning you may have to do won't be worth the effort.

When you're pruning, think about what you want to do with the plant in winter; you may want to groom it for a particular spot indoors.

PESTS AND DISEASES

Tropical gardens have the same pests and diseases you find in any garden. The key to healthy plants is keeping them free from stress. Good growing practices and a brief but forceful shower every few days usually take care of any insects, eggs, or disease spores.

OTHER SUMMER CHORES

Sprucing up the garden during the growing season entails cutting flowers to encourage growth, removing fading flowers, and pulling up dead annuals.

DEADHEADING Removing dead flowers is easy, and it makes a big difference in the appearance of the garden and the length of the blooming period.

Collecting bouquets often improves growth. Cutting the foliage of Persian shield *(Strobilanthes dyeranus)* and silver dollar eucalyptus *(Eucalyptus cinerea)* frequently encourages the plants to send out bright new growth. Pick hibiscus blooms daily for your home. Though flowers last only a day, they brighten any space and require no water.

REMOVING SPENT ANNUALS Once most annuals have set seeds, the show is over. Removing prolific self-sowers before they set seeds prevents them from swamping you with volunteer seedlings and keeps your garden neat. Climate changes may also affect some annuals. Nasturtiums and petunias, for example, die back when summer comes to warm climates, torenias and portulaca when the weather is cold.

ABOVE: *Don't try to deadhead plants when abundance makes it difficult. Most of those angel's trumpets* (Brugmansia) *will drop on their own. Design: Bob Clark* LEFT: *Picking dahlias keeps plants blooming.*

Winter Care

Even in tropical climes, certain plants go dormant in winter, but good summer care—and age—can make plants more cold hardy. Some plants die to the ground but come back from the roots; others must be replaced. Knowledgeable gardeners keep material handy to cover tender plants on cold nights or trundle containers indoors. When plants are too big to move, they can be tipped over and covered to protect the roots.

TOP: *Dig carefully to avoid damage.*
CENTER: *Wash, dry, spray, and loosely wrap cannas for storage.*
BOTTOM: *Save tiny gladiolus bulblets; they grow to blooming size in two to three years.*

SAVING SEEDS

Saving seeds works well for many annuals. Gathering seeds as they ripen and before they are dispersed from the pod is the easiest way to guarantee new plants the next year. Put the seeds in envelopes and label them with the name, height, color, and other pertinent information, such as where they grew best. But remember that seedling plants have two parents, so the resulting plants may differ in color or size from the original. Keep seeds in a cool, dry place until you're ready to plant them. To get the best growth, you may want to start seeds indoors in late winter, weeks before you set young plants outdoors.

TAKING CUTTINGS

When plants are too big to move or cover, taking cuttings is one of the best ways to preserve them (see page 56). Check the plant encyclopedia, beginning on page 87, for plants that can be saved with the least amount of work and worry. You can pot cuttings once they are rooted and take more cuttings from the original ones as spring approaches. Plants from cuttings always have the same characteristics as the one parent plant.

DIGGING AND STORING BULBS

Most tropical plants that form bulbs, corms, or other tuberous roots go dormant with the onset of cool or dry weather or with the first frost. If you live in an area where the ground does not freeze or in a marginal zone where layers of mulch keep it from freezing, bulbs can stay in the ground. Cool-climate gardeners, however, have long been digging up gladiolus, caladiums, cannas, and dahlias; other tropicals only add to the list.

There are several ways to store bulbs. You can wash off the soil to remove any insects or disease spores and then allow bulbs to air-dry. Using an antidesiccant spray curtails moisture loss and prevents fungal attack. Wrap each bulb loosely in newspaper and store in an opaque bag. Or you can put bulbs in a tray of peat moss, bark chips, or sawdust. Some gardeners prefer to leave soil around the bulbs to keep them from drying out; others pile them in boxes and cover

Divide rhizomatous clumps like those of this iris into sections.

are well fed and well watered. So you will have roots to divide after digging in the fall or before replanting in the spring. As a rule, bulbs, corms, and fibrous roots separate easily, though you may have to cut apart tubers and rhizomes. Just be sure that each section of tuber you cut has an eye or growing point.

with a sheet of plastic, or dry them upside-down in the sun and dust with fungicidal powder before storing.

However you prepare them, keep dormant bulbs in a dark place where temperatures range from 35 to 50°F/2 to 10°C. Check them once a month, and spray with water if they seem to be shriveling. Discard or cut away any sign of rot. Six weeks to a month before the last expected frost, plant the bulbs in pots or trays in a warm, bright place to restart growth. When it's warm enough to set them out, the plants will be weeks ahead in both size and flowering.

DIVIDING THE BOUNTY Most bulbs multiply underground during the growing season, especially if plants

INDOOR DORMANCY

Many tropical plants go dormant naturally; others can be forced into dormancy by withholding water and keeping them in a cool, dark place with temperatures above 35°F/2°C in winter. If plants are not already in containers, put them in clean pots or wrap their root balls tightly

A dark, frost-free basement, garage, or closet is an ideal place for dormant tropicals to overwinter. You can keep more plants with less work and worry, and they will make a quicker and larger impact in the next year's garden.

In areas of marginal hardiness, a deep layer of mulch will often protect tender perennials and bulbs.

temperatures are cool. When spring arrives, plants may start to grow. Gradually introduce more light, heat, and water as garden reentry approaches.

OUTDOOR PROTECTION

For plants left in the ground, water well before the soil freezes. Much cold damage is due to dryness, since the roots' water uptake is reduced in cool weather while winter winds and bright sunshine continue to take away moisture. Unless it rains regularly all winter in your area, provide plants with a few buckets of warm (not hot) water two or three times between late December and mid-February. Using an antidesiccant spray on leaves and stems also reduces dryness (see "Helpful Plant Products" at right).

MULCHING AND MOUNDING Where soils seldom freeze more than a few inches down, some herbaceous perennials and bulbs can be cut back to the ground and covered with a deep layer of mulch to keep the roots from freezing. Even in warmer climates, gardeners mound up soil around the graft points of citrus and other fruit trees so that if the top of the plant is frozen in a cold snap, the new growth will be the grafted variety, not the rootstock's.

in plastic and place them in buckets or boxes.

Herbaceous plants, even trees and shrubs grown as perennials, can stay outside until a frost withers their leaves, and then be cut back to 10 inches above the soil. Woody plants must be taken in before a frost. Cut them back only enough to get them inside; any remaining leaves will gradually turn yellow and drop.

Check dormant plants every 2 weeks during the winter to be sure the soil is just wet enough that it does not shrink away from the roots and the sides of the container. If it's dry down to 2 inches, add a little water. Water needs to be added only every 2 to 4 weeks as long as

Helpful Plant Products

The following products are optional plant aids.

Antidesiccant spray, a biodegradable waxy substance that settles over plants like an invisible plastic wrap, retards moisture loss; some contain fungicide. Sprays are used to reduce wilting when transplanting. They may also help marginal plants make it through the winter by reducing water loss from leaves and stems. The sprays, available in garden centers and through catalogs, won't harm plants or stop photosynthesis. You can buy them in ready-to-use spray form or in concentrate. Follow directions, one of which will be to use them when temperatures are above 40°F/4°C. They do wash off with continued rain, so consider spraying again in mid-December and mid-January, or whenever there is a thaw.

Natural hormones that stimulate root development and prevent rot are useful when rooting cuttings. You can also buy a root stimulant that prevents transplant shock and soak your plant in it before or during planting. Products that add enzymes to the soil may be helpful for plant growth, resistance to diseases and pests, and protection against cold-weather damage.

CAGING AND WRAPPING Making a cage around a plant and filling it with mulch is one of the best ways to provide winter protection. Wait until a light frost sends the plant into dormancy, which makes it more cold tolerant, before spraying the plant's stems and leaves with a broad-spectrum fungicide to prevent diseases. Then put the cage (or other type of container for colder climates) over the plant and fill it with a loose pile of mulch—pine needles, leaves, or straw. This will permit air circulation, reduce the light level, and insulate the plant. The slow decomposition of the mulch will also produce some heat around the plant.

Larger plants may require wrapping. Again, wait until after a light frost before applying a fungicide. Depending on your climate and the cold spell, a single layer of burlap may do the job. If you need several layers of protection, place sticks around the plant to keep the cloth or plastic from touching it. Loosely piling a layer of straw around the plant and tying it with string before covering it with a sheet of opaque plastic allows the plant to breathe, prevents moisture from condensing on the branches, and holds the plastic away from the plant. To hold in heat and keep the wrap from blowing away, fasten the lower edges of the plastic sheet to the ground with mulch, rocks, or U-shaped pins made from coat hangers. Then add a layer of burlap or cloth to camouflage the plastic.

You may need to ventilate wrapped plants during warm spells to keep them from roasting. The best way is to leave a flap at one side of the base that can be turned back in warm weather and resealed in cold.

LEFT: *A fig tree sleeps in this leaf-filled wire cage.* CENTER: *A solid cage offers more protection.* BELOW: *When wrapped with straw, plastic, and burlap, Japanese banana (Musa basjoo) may survive 20 degrees more cold than if left exposed to wind and weather.*

Miniature greenhouses can be lowered into place and pinned to the ground so that they won't blow away. Be sure to provide and use an opening flap for ventilation, or tip covers back on warmer days. On the coldest nights, lights can be added inside and blankets spread over the tops of these shelters.

Living with Snow

Snow can act as an insulator. Temperatures under just a few inches of snow can be as much as 30°F/17°C warmer than air temperature. In most cases, it's best to leave snow where it falls or carefully bank it higher around marginally hardy plants during very cold weather. You run the risk of breaking branches if you try to remove it.

TIPPING AND DITCHING If you live where temperatures remain below 0°F/-18°C for long periods, ditching is safer than wrapping. Before the soil freezes, remove any foliage and dig a trench on one side of the plant. Then loosen the roots on the other side and tip the plant into the trench, being careful to bend only the roots, not the trunk. Cover the plant with soil and then mulch (see the illustration below). In spring, carefully reverse the process, pulling the plant up straight and reburying the loosened roots.

MINIATURE GREENHOUSES Instead of wrapping a plant, you can make a miniature greenhouse that retains heat and keeps out wind and water. Simply cover a wood frame with a double layer of plastic sheeting, leaving some overlap at ground level, and fasten the plastic to the frame with staples or nails. Make the enclosure large enough to keep plant leaves from touching the plastic and sturdy enough to withstand the elements. In areas of heavy snow, slant the structure top enough to keep snow from piling up. Lower the greenhouse

over the plant and secure the sheeting to the ground with mulch or pins, leaving a flap to open for ventilation as needed.

LIGHT AND HEAT When winter temperatures drop, many businesses and parks generate a few degrees of heat by wrapping small decorative lights around plants. In a miniature greenhouse you can add incandescent lighting and a blanket cover on the coldest nights. If you use light for heat, make sure that bulbs don't touch the plants or any flammable materials. The lights should be plugged into an external outlet with a ground-fault circuit. Low-wattage cables used to keep water pipes from freezing provide another form of heat. They can be entwined among the insulating material of a wrapped plant or wrapped around a root ball during planting, and activated during cold spells.

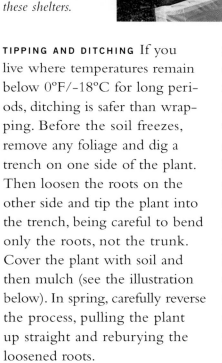

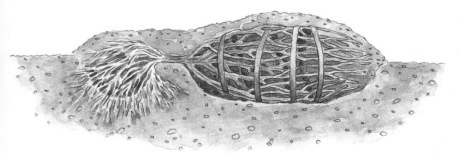

CHAPTER SIX

A Tropical Sampler

THE SELECTION OF TROPICAL PLANTS shown in the pages that follow includes the most treasured specimens, the easiest to find, and, most important, the easiest to grow. All of these plants can spend the entire summer outdoors, anywhere in the United States or southern Canada. And they can stay in the garden year-round in the zones listed with each entry. So let these fascinating plants turn your garden into a tropical showplace with minimum work and worry. ❧ Once you've sampled these suggestions, you'll have the knowledge and confidence to explore other tropical species and cultivars. Leaf through catalogs, browse in nurseries and public gardens, chat with fellow gardeners in warm-weather climes, and gather seeds and cuttings as you travel.

ACALYPHA

ZONES 24, 25, 27; H1, H2

Eye-catching evergreen shrubs grow 2 to 3 feet a season. Red flowers are showy tassels, up to 18 inches long on the chenille plant *(A. hispida)* and the smaller, trailing *A. repens.* Copper leaf *(A. wilkesiana)* has smaller tassels but longer leaves with variegated foliage in combinations of red, green, and pink, and of green and white. All are frost-tender even in warmer climates but usually come back from roots. Grow in full sun to partial shade, keep soil evenly moist, and feed twice a month. You can overwinter as a houseplant in bright light. Bring plant inside before night temperatures fall below 50°F/10°C. Cuttings root easily.

Acalypha hispida

Agave americana 'Marginata'

AGAVE

ZONES VARY BY SPECIES

These evergreen succulent perennials have stemless whorls of fleshy, strap-shaped leaves. The sculptural century plant *(A. americana:* zones 10, 12–30; H1, H2) has gray blue to green leaves with stripes of yellow or white; they are wickedly spiny on the edges and ends. Century plants grow slowly up to 10 feet and seldom flower, some supposedly waiting 100 years to blossom. After four to five years, the plant may send up a giant stalk that looks like an asparagus spear. When its yellowish green blooms die, so do that stem and whorls but not the pups around them. Plant these Southwest natives in full sun in a large container with sandy, well-drained soil; feed lightly. Winter as a houseplant in a sunny window; or you can let it go dormant, put in a cool place with some light, and water monthly. Divide pups.

Allamanda cathartica

ALLAMANDA

ZONES 23–27; H1, H2

This handsome evergreen vine grows up to 50 feet a year in the tropics and will reach 3 to 4 feet in a cool climate. It blooms almost nonstop. *A. cathartica* 'Hendersonii' has orange yellow trumpet-shaped flowers as long as 6 inches and glossy green foliage. *A. blanchetii* has purplish pink trumpets with darker throats. *A. schottii* is a shrub that is easy to grow in cool climates and carry over the winter with cuttings. Plant in full sun; keep soil moist in the growing season, almost dry in winter. Feed weekly in summer. Plant is poisonous if ingested; milky sap can irritate skin. Vines are difficult houseguests; if you don't have a greenhouse, try taking cuttings or buy new plants the following spring.

ALOCASIA, COLOCASIA esculenta, XANTHOSOMA

Elephant's ear, taro

ZONES VARY BY GENUS

These perennial cousins are noted for huge, arrow-shaped leaves with bold textures and attention-grabbing colors: green to almost-black burgundy plus striking variegations of green, white, and purple. All are quick growers and heavy feeders. They prefer wet places (some even grow in water) and need protection from wind. Divide as needed and cut yellowing leaves to the ground. *Alocasia* (zones 22–27; H1, H2) likes full to partial shade; *Colocasia* (zones 12, 16–28; H1, H2) and *Xanthosoma* (zones 12, 13, 16, 17, 21–27; H1, H2) prefer full sun to partial shade. Cultivars are sold as dormant corms or potted plants. Overwinter as a houseplant in cool climates if you can provide plenty of humidity. Or let it go dormant and store. In-ground plants can be dug up and stored with dormant bulbs.

Alocasia × amazonica

Aloe striata

ALOE

ZONES 8, 9, 12–27; H1

This attractive, useful succulent has fleshy, pointed gray green or mottled leaves with spiny edges. Its gel soothes and helps heal burns, wounds, and bug bites. Some species grow as trees in the tropics and can become shrubs in California. Most species are small with clusters of orange, yellow, red, or cream flowers that bloom in flushes throughout the summer. Easy to grow indoors or out, the tough, highly drought-tolerant plant prefers full sun but will take partial shade. Move gradually from shade to sun or from indoors to outdoors. Feed and water sparingly. Good container plant and houseplant.

ALTERNANTHERA

ALL ZONES AS ANNUAL AND
HOUSEPLANT; H1, H2 AS
PERENNIAL

This very colorful, low-growing foliage plant makes ground-covering waves around bases of taller and long-stemmed plants, such as bananas and gingers, or cascades over containers. *A. dentata* and *A. polygonoides* are sprawlers; parrotleaf (*A. ficoidea*) is a more compact mounding type. Their taller and more robust cousins *Amaranthus* and *Iresine* often bear the same common names (Joseph's coat, bloodleaf, and calico plant). Colors are richer in full sun, but plants also do well in partial shade. Provide plenty of water, not too much food. All make good houseplants, blooming with small, cloverlike flowers in fall and winter. Take cuttings in late summer before buds set.

Alternanthera ficoidea 'Brilliantissima'

Anthurium andraeanum

ANTHURIUM
Spathe flower
ZONES 25; H2

These exotic plants, known for their large green leaves and lush flower bracts in vivid red, luscious pink, or white, are no harder to grow than some orchids in warm areas with high humidity. Strap flowers (*A. crystallinum*) have large, velvety leaves with prominent veins and less showy flowers. Plants bloom best in partial shade but are sensitive to cold and drafts. They can reach 4 feet if they're planted in an epiphytic orchid mix and receive constant moisture. Fertilize once a month. Place a potted plant in the branches of a tree for the ultimate layered look. If you have a place with high humidity away from direct sun, plant can spend winter indoors. Or start anew from divisions, cuttings, or seeds.

ANTIGONON leptopus
Coral vine, queen's wreath
ZONES 12, 13, 18–30; H1, H2

Native to Mexico and wild in warm climates, this quick-climbing vine has bright sprays of 6 to 20 delicate flowers from midsummer to fall in a shade of rose pink that lifts the heart. Varieties also include a rare white 'Album' and hot rose pink 'Baja Red'. Leaves are bright green, heart or arrow shaped, and 3 to 5 inches long. Vine needs full sun but withstands dry conditions, low humidity, and cool temperatures. To show off blooms, plant vine in a container against a trellis. If overfertilized, it grows no flowers. Leave tuberous roots in the ground in a well-mulched site where winter temperatures don't go below 25°F/−4°C. In colder climes, cut vine back to the base and put in dormant storage. Start from cuttings, seeds, or bulbs.

Antigonon leptopus

Aphelandra squarrosa

APHELANDRA squarrosa
ZONES 23–25, 27; H1, H2

This favorite houseplant does well in shade outdoors at the front of a border or in a container. Its 8-inch leaves have sunken veins of silvery white. Plants bloom with 6-inch spikes of small flowers peeking from showy bracts of yellow, orange, or red that last into fall. Prefers moist, acid soil and warm nights. Repot plant before first frost and move inside into bright filtered light. Take cuttings in late winter to late spring.

BAMBOO
ZONES VARY BY SPECIES

Used for food, fuel, and construction, bamboo is called "friend of the people" by the Chinese and "gift of the gods" by Colombians. Comprising more than 70 genera and 2,400 species, these giant grasses make a good garden accent or screen. They even add a musical sound when shoots rub or creak together and leaves rustle in the breeze. Shoots, called "culms," grow to their full height (up to 30 feet) in a single season. Canes are green, brown, gold, or black; leaves can be variegated. Most bamboo takes full sun to light shade. For rapid growth, water frequently and feed once a month with high-nitrogen or lawn fertilizer. To restrict size, feed and water less. Bamboo spreads by clumping or by running; runners must be contained, as they are highly invasive.

Though many bamboos are tropical and subtropical, some of the best cold-hardy species are the clumping fountain bamboo *(Fargesia nitida)* and umbrella bamboo *(F. murielae)*. They can reach up to 12 feet tall and are evergreen where winters dip to −25°F/−32°C. Black bamboo *(Phyllostachys nigra),* leaf hardy to 0°F/−18° and root hardy as much as 10 degrees lower, is a runner so beautiful with its black stems and jade foliage that many find it worth the trouble of containing. Some bamboos survive for a time indoors, but it's best to plant a cold-hardy type.

Phyllostachys nigra

BEGONIA

ALL ZONES AS ANNUAL;
ZONES 14–28, H1, H2 (EXCEPT
AS NOTED) AS PERENNIAL

Begonias come in a wide range of forms, sizes, and foliage and flower colors. All have two kinds of flowers: large, male flowers with yellow stamens and smaller female flowers. Most plants prefer partial to light shade and rich, moist soil. Fertilize every other week with a half-strength solution. Groups have similar care needs and growth habits. Propagate plants by leaf, stem, or root cuttings or by seeds. Wait until the appearance of pointed leaves, which indicate the direction in which the flowers will grow, before planting.

Cane-type, or angel-wing, begonias have tall, woody stems with bamboolike joints. Many have variegated or colored foliage. Plants bloom from early spring through autumn. Protect plants from wind and bring indoors when temperatures cool. In early spring when old canes are bare, shorten to two leaf joints.

Hardy begonias grow as 2- to 3-foot-tall perennials in zones 3–24. Branching red stems carry large, smooth, coppery green leaves with red undersides and drooping clusters of pink or white flowers in summer. Tops die down after frost; mulch to protect roots.

Rex *(B. × rex)* and rhizomatous begonias grow in large, low clumps with bold, multicolored leaves. Some flower in winter through summer. Plants need high humidity but require water only when the top inch or so of soil is dry. Overwinter as a houseplant in a slightly larger container.

Bedding, or wax, begonias, with small, round green or bronze leaves and white, orange, pink, or red flowers, are widely available in garden centers. Some grow only 6 to 8 inches; others may reach 10 to 12 inches. Most

Angel-wing Begonia

will withstand full sun in cooler climates. Don't overwater.

Tuberous begonias (zones 23, 24; H1) are magnificent large-flowered hybrids. They range from plants with saucer-size blooms and a few upright succulent stems to multistemmed cascading sorts covered in blossoms. Most are summer and fall bloomers (winter and spring in warm climates); flowers are in every color but blue. Uprights bloom more profusely. Shapes are frilly (like that of a carnation), formal double (like a camellia's), and tight-centered (like a rose's).

Most gardeners buy dormant tubers in midwinter and plant them about 4 inches apart in pots or trays. Grow in rich, moist but not soggy soil in filtered light. Keep them warm (above 65°F/18°C). Plant outside when tubers have two leaves and temperatures are above 50°F/10°C. You can also plant tubers in the ground, amending soil with potting mix. For best bloom, mist often with water. When leaves wilt and yellow in fall, reduce watering and stop feeding. When leaves fall, lift tubers, shake off soil, and dry in a cool spot over winter.

Bougainvillea glabra 'Variegata'

BOUGAINVILLEA

ZONES 5, 6, 12–17, 19, 21–29; H1, H2

One of the most popular blooming tropical vines or sprawling shrubs, bougainvillea has bright green heart-shaped leaves and wicked thorns. Large, papery, vibrantly colored flower bracts grow in great profusion from spring into winter. Color varies with the amount of sun; white- and yellow-flowered varieties need light shade in the hottest climates. Double-flowered types can look messy because they hold faded blooms a long time.

Prune after flowering in warm climates, in early spring after danger of frost in marginal areas, and during the growing season as needed. Propagate with cuttings. To minimize shock to sensitive roots when planting, cut off container bottom; set pot and plant in the hole; and then slide pot up over plant, filling in with soil as you go. Tie shoots to a sturdy support so that they won't whip in wind. Fertilize when growing season begins and again in early summer. Water regularly in spring, moderately during bloom period. In cold climates, keep in containers and overwinter in a greenhouse or sunroom, or store dormant in a cool, dark basement or garage.

BREYNIA nivosa

Snow bush

ZONES 22–27; H1, H2

This evergreen shrub grows to 3 or 4 feet tall and wide with gracefully arching dark red branches and thin oval leaves; flowers are inconspicuous. It's stunning in combination with burgundy coleus or red-leafed cannas. Most commonly seen variety is 'Roseopicta' (sweet pea bush or calico plant), with mottled leaves of red, pink, white, and green. *B. n. nana* has pure white new growth on red stems; *B. n.* 'Thimma' offers yellow-and-green variegated leaves. Snow bush does well in part shade to full sun. Plant offers best color in sun with rich soil kept evenly moist. Feed monthly in spring and summer; prune occasionally to encourage new stems and more colorful leaves. Overwinter in a greenhouse or take stem cuttings in spring and summer, semiripe-wood stem cuttings or root cuttings in winter. Does not do well as a houseplant, as leaves drop in low humidity.

Breynia nivosa 'Roseopicta'

Clockwise from top left: Neoregelia carolinae 'Tricolor', Guzmania, Tillandsia, Aechmea fasciata 'Morgana'

BROMELIADS

ZONES VARY BY GENUS

There are 45 genera and more than 2,000 species of bromeliads, with pineapple being the best known. Most of these rain forest natives are perennials with clustered leaves and showy flowers. They grow in trees or on rocks, and their roots anchor them, so their main source of water is what collects in their vaselike whorls.

Leaves may be handsomely marked; flowers are bright spikes or candelabra that gain beauty from colorful, often long-lasting bracts. Some plants have attractive berries. A few (*Puya* is the best known) are terrestrial desert plants that resemble yuccas and thrive in the same conditions.

Most grow best in partial to light shade, although a few, especially ones with slender, hairy, leathery leaves, tolerate full sun. Feed monthly with half-strength fertilizer solution. Increase by separating pups when they are one-third the size of the parent or by collecting seeds. They make excellent houseplants if kept in containers with a well-draining soil mix; overwatering causes rotting. Indoors, bromeliads like high humidity and bright light.

AECHMEA

ZONES 22–27; H1, H2

Leaf whorls grow up to 3 feet long and are often marked with crossbands of silver, pink, red, or burgundy. Small flowers come from clusters of bright pink, orange, or red bracts that last for months, some followed by berries. *A. fasciata,* called silver vase plant, has silvery scales that fall off to leave green bands on lilac gray leaves; white, woolly stems hold dense clusters of bluish purple or red flowers with rosy pink bracts.

ANANAS
Pineapple
ZONES 24–27; H1, H2

This group includes species bearing the familiar edible fruit, as well as some highly ornamental plants 3 to 5 feet tall and 2 to 4 feet wide with long, narrow, often spiny leaves. Named varieties have different coloration. 'Tricolor' is the brightest, with leaves striped in green, yellow, and red. The bright pink and blue flowers first form in the center of the cluster but soon grow high on a sturdy stem. Start plants from pups or pineapple tops, and plant in full sun. If you move the plant in during winter and out in summer, it may take several years to bear fruit.

BILLBERGIA
ZONES 12–14, 15 (WITH PROTECTION), 16–27; H1, H2

Spectacular bromeliads grow in basal rosettes of stiff, spiny evergreen leaves colored green, red, or silver. They spread quickly and bloom with showy, drooping clusters of red, pink, or blue flowers. Queen's tears *(B. nutans)* has silvery bronze leaves and blue-edged apple green flowers spilling out of rosy bracts. Plants take partial sun outdoors.

CRYPTANTHUS ZONATUS
ZONES 17, 23, 24; H1, H2

Grown for its showy foliage, perennial has bright whorls of pink to dark red leaves banded crosswise with green, brown, or white. Plant grows 12 to 18 inches wide and less than a foot tall.

GUZMANIA
ZONES 25; H2

Natives of the Andean rain forest, these popular low-growers have glossy green or variegated lance-shaped leaves. They bloom in summer with small white or yellow flowers in a large cluster of pointed yellow, red, or orange bracts on thick stalks. Give them shade, moist soil, and high humidity; bring in when nights fall below 60°F/16°C.

NEOREGELIA
ZONES 21–27; H1, H2

Tight clusters of wide leathery leaves are often strikingly colored or marked, most with brightly colored centers of pink, magenta, red, or orange; flowers are less conspicuous. Painted fingernail plant *(N. spectabilis)* has olive green leaves with red tips. Plants are low-growing.

TILLANDSIA
ZONES 22–27

These unusual bromeliads grow without soil. The familiar Spanish moss *(T. usneoides)* has gray, threadlike foliage that dangles from oak trees throughout the southern United States. Some have colorful bracts and flowers on short stems that bloom in spring or fall. Since plants get their moisture from the air, high humidity is important.

BRUGMANSIA (DATURA)
Angel's trumpet
ZONES 12, 13, 16–27; H1, H2

Of all the easy-to-grow plants, these have perhaps the largest and loveliest flowers. The pendulous trumpets, as much as 12 inches long and 8 inches across in white, yellow, pink, or peach, have a heavenly fragrance in most species. Peak bloom occurs in summer and fall. When the flowers fall, smooth seedpods remain. All parts of the plant are poisonous if ingested. Plants quickly become large shrubs or small trees with an umbrella of large green leaves. Does best in full sun to light shade. Feed every 2 weeks and keep it well watered. Dormant plants can overwinter inside in low light with very little water. Prune roots and repot in spring, or take cuttings to keep on a windowsill.

Brugmansia

CALADIUM bicolor
Fancy-leafed caladium
ZONES 25–27; H2

Large delicate-looking but sturdy leaves will brighten shady spots from spring until frost with mounds of color from almost pure white edged in dark green to mottled patterns of green, pink, peach, red, and white. Varieties vary from 8 to 24 inches tall. Buy tubers in spring or dig and store bulbs over the winter. If potted in March with the knobby side up and tops even with the soil surface, you'll get larger plants and a longer season. Otherwise, plant outdoors in rich humus-enhanced soil when nighttime temperatures are reliably warm (above 60°F/16°C). Keep plants moist. Most caladiums need some shade; some will take deep shade. Newer hybrids with narrower leaves and darker colors will thrive in full sun with enough water. Fertilize weekly; remove flowers, as they encourage tubers to go dormant. Overwinter container plants in dormant storage.

Caladium bicolor 'White Queen'

Canna 'Tropicanna'

CANNA
ZONES 6–9, 12–31; H1, H2

Old-fashioned cannas offer large and often colorful foliage, stately form, and showy flowers. Colorful blossoms range from near-white through orange to red; some are bicolored. Foliage may be brighter than the blooms, providing constant color from late spring until frost. Place cannas in groups of three to five in the middle or back of a garden bed, depending on their height (1½ to 6 feet). Plant tubers in full sun, 6 inches deep and 1 to 2 feet apart in soil enriched with humus. Cannas thrive in wet places; some can even live in water. Feed monthly with liquid plant food. Cut back stalks when blooms fade to encourage new flowers unless you prefer the foliage. Where the soil doesn't freeze, leave tubers in the ground, or dig them up and store after frost blackens the tops. Divide in spring or fall. Plant outdoors after the last frost; for a head start, in March plant them in containers indoors, and then move them out when warm weather comes.

CHLOROPHYTUM comosum
Spider plant
ZONES 15–17, 19–27; H1, H2

Spider plants grow indoors or out, as a ground cover or foliage plant. They are attractive if planted in the ground but show to best advantage in hanging baskets or elevated containers. Some plants have solid green leaves, but most have thin arching leaves with white or yellow stripes. Stems are tipped by small white, star-shaped blooms followed by little plantlets that dangle well below the parent plant. Best grown in partial to dense shade, plants can acclimate to full sun in cooler climates. Though fairly drought tolerant, plants need weekly watering and monthly feeding. Bring containers in on frosty nights or overwinter as houseplants. Spider plants are easily propagated by rooting plantlets or dividing the parent.

Chlorophytum comosum

Citrus sinensis

CITRUS

ZONES 8, 9, 12–27, H1, H2 FOR
MOST; 7, 28–31 FOR HARDIEST

Citrus trees are attractive all
year, with glossy foliage, 3 to
4 weeks of fragrant flowers, and
months of delicious fruit. The
leaves are aromatic if crushed.
Where temperatures seldom fall
below freezing, citrus does well,
increasing in hardiness as it
matures. In marginally hardy
zones, plant trees in frost-protected
spots. Citrus does best in full
sun, though it tolerates partial
shade in warm climates. Water
when the soil surface dries out.
Don't overwater or mulch around
the trunk, as citrus is susceptible
to root rot.

Citrus in containers can be
moved indoors or to a greenhouse in cold weather. Move
plants gradually—over at least 3
or 4 weeks. Water less in winter,
allowing the soil to dry out.
Fertilize very lightly until
4 weeks before the move outdoors. Provide plenty of natural
or artificial light and plenty of
humidity. Keep plant away from
heat and drafts, mist frequently,
and ring with pebble-filled trays
of water.

Choose the hardiest plants:
lemons, limes, kumquats
('Meiwa' is sweet and delicious),
and calamondin (sour-acid
mandarin). A shrubby mandarin
hybrid, 'Yuzu', with mildly sweet,
lemon-flavored fruit, fares well
where temperatures are as
low as 10°F/–12°C or below.
'Thomasville', an orangequat, is
a small tree with limelike fruit
that is hardy to about 0°F/–18°C.
Orange hybrids 'Morton' and
'US-119' taste much like a tart
orange and are hardy to 5°F/
–15°C or below.

CLERODENDRUM

ZONES VARY BY SPECIES

This highly diverse genus includes
vines and shrubs with vividly
colored, fantastic flowers. Bleeding
heart glorybower vine (C. thomsoniae: zones 22–28; H1, H2) has
clusters of red and white blooms.
Pagoda flower (C. paniculatum:
zones 25, 26) has showy pyramids
of scarlet flowers. C. wallichii
(zones 25, 26) has spectacular
pendants of white flowers.
Butterfly bush (C. myricoides
'Ugandense': zones 9, 14–29) has
lovely spires of light blue flowers.

Plants start easily from seeds
or cuttings, grow 4 to 6 feet tall
the first season, and have large
leaves. Grow in full sun to partial
shade in moist, slightly acid soil
enriched with humus. Water
well and feed twice monthly.
Tie up vine stems. Overwinter
as cuttings, or move to a greenhouse or sunny room. If space
is a problem, you can induce
dormancy and keep containers
in the basement or garage (see
page 82).

Clerodendrum thomsoniae

CODIAEUM variegatum 'Pictum'
Croton

ZONES 24–27; H1, H2

Crotons are grown primarily for their large, leathery, glossy leaves in many shapes and brilliant colors that range from almost pure white to yellow, orange, pink, red, and crimson. Leaf colors vary with placement and amount of sun; some varieties do best in shade. It is important to know the plant's cultivar name and preference before choosing your garden site, as crotons dislike being transplanted.

Crotons root fairly easily from cuttings or air layering. Although drought tolerant, they do best if watered once a week in winter and more often in summer. Keeping the soil moist helps plants survive cold weather. Feed weekly during spring and summer. Avoid legginess by pinching back the growing tips of new shoots when they are only a few inches long (some varieties bush naturally without pinching). Overwinter as houseplants or take cuttings. Bring inside when nights get down to 50°F/10°C.

Codiaeum variegatum 'Pictum'

Coleus × hybridus

COLEUS × hybridus

ALL ZONES AS ANNUAL OR HOUSEPLANT; 24, H1, H2 AS PERENNIAL

These pretty plants are grown for their dramatically colored leaves in a rainbow of color combinations from almost white to almost black. Most kinds grow to 3 feet, but some dwarf varieties stay under 10 inches and make a fine ground cover. Removing the spikes of light blue flowers adds strength to the foliage. Coleus blends well with ferns and usually thrives in the same shady conditions, although some new cultivars do well in sun. The new sun lovers mature so slowly that they don't bloom for a year or two, which prevents them from getting lanky. Coleus prefers moist soil and regular feeding with high-nitrogen fertilizer. Pinch stems often to encourage branching, and shear back plants in sun by one-third in midsummer. Coleus makes an excellent houseplant. Bring plants or cuttings indoors before a frost threatens. Coleus roots quickly and easily, even in water. Growing from seed is easy but takes longer.

CORDYLINE

ZONES VARY BY SPECIES

Woody plant with swordlike leaves makes a bright focal point in a tropical garden. Mature plants with long, slender trunks may bloom with spires of fragrant flowers. Giant dracaena (*C. australis:* zones 5, 8, 14–27; H1, H2) is the hardiest, down to 15°F/–9°C. Upper leaves are erect; lower ones arch. Plants can grow 5 to 25 feet tall, climbing 2 to 3 feet in a season. Needs full sun and deep soil for carrot-like roots. Cut back when young for multiple trunks. Ti plant (*C. fruticosa:* zones 21–25, 27; H1, H2) has red, yellow, or variegated leaves and footlong white or red flower clusters; it's hardy to 26°F/–3°C.

Plants grow in full sun to partial shade in rich soil. Keep moist during the growing season, drier in winter. If leaf tips brown, add more water. Feed every 2 weeks during active growth. Take cuttings often or use in bouquets to encourage bright new growth and compact shape. Cuttings root easily from stem ends or pieces.

Cordyline fruticosa

Crinum amabile

CRINUM

ZONES 8, 9, 12–31, 33 (WARMER PARTS); H1, H2

Noted for their lush foliage and lilylike flowers, these tropical beauties can grow to 5 feet in a single season. Thick stems rise from long, broad, straplike leaves, each bearing a cluster of long-stalked flowers. Showy blossoms may be pure white, striped with claret red, or tinged with rose purple; many are wonderfully fragrant. Most species bloom in spring or summer, year-round in Hawaii. Bulbs are available year-round, but spring and fall are the best planting times. Prefers rich soil with room to grow, and plenty of water and food in summer. Propagates easily from offsets or from seeds. In cool climates, plants can spend the winter in a cool, bright spot indoors. Or leave them outdoors until frost kills the tops, and store as dormant bulbs.

CROSSANDRA
infundibuliformis

Firecracker flower

ZONES 25, H2; MARGINAL IN 26, H1

An evergreen perennial, this small shrub blooms almost constantly with red, pink, salmon, or orange flowers. Plant in full sun and combine with a russet-foliaged plant. It likes acid soil, ample water, and monthly feeding. Overwinter as a houseplant on a sunny windowsill, or take cuttings for the following year.

Crossandra infundibuliformis

Cuphea ignea 'David Verity'

CUPHEA
ZONES 16–29; H1, H2

Provides color throughout warm months. Species and cultivars vary considerably, but reliability and constant bloom characterize all. Cigar plant (*C. ignea:* zones 11–13, 16–24; H1, H2) has inch-long tubular flowers, which have a flared lip and end in a grayish ring, like a tiny cigar with glowing ash. Most plants stay small, up to 2 feet, with bright red, orange red, white, peach, or pink flowers. *C. micropetala* is hardy into North Carolina and grows to 3 to 5 feet. It has deep red stems, green leaves, and orange, yellow, and white flowers. Bat-faced cuphea (*C. llavea:* zones 11–13, 21–24; H1, H2) has blooms resembling dark purple faces with tiny bright-red ears. False heather *(C. hyssopifolia)* has small leaves and hundreds of tiny, round, six-petaled lavender flowers that look like heather. Use in small beds, as a border edging along paths, or in containers.

Grow any of these species in full sun. They prefer moist soil but won't suffer from slight dryness. Feed weekly and cut back if plants get leggy. Overwinter as houseplants in a cool, sunny window; store as dormant plants in a cool, dark basement or garage; or treat as an annual.

CYCAS
Cycads
ZONES VARY BY SPECIES

Neither ferns nor true palms, these shrub-size evergreens are primitive cone-bearing relatives of conifers, excellent for tropical effects. Spiral clusters of finely cut, leathery, dark green branches arch gracefully from the tops of low trunks. They can grow slowly—only a few inches a year—and are often as wide as tall. The fruits on the female cone have smooth red to orange egg-shaped seeds. Queen sago (*C. circinalis:* zones 23–27; H1, H2) has much larger leaves than sago palm (*C. revoluta:* zones 8–29; H1, H2) and is less hardy. Related *Dioon* and *Zamia* species are similar though smaller, with rounded leaflets in deep green to gray blue. Plant cycads in full

Cycas revoluta

sun to light shade in well-drained but evenly moist soil. Feed in spring and midsummer. All are prone to scale; sago palm can suffer from potassium deficiency. All have high drought tolerance. Propagate from seeds or from offshoots. Overwinter indoors or in a greenhouse, and let them dry out between waterings. Harden off carefully when moving inside and out.

Cymbopogon citratus

CYMBOPOGON citratus
Lemon grass
ZONES 12, 13, 16, 17, 23–27;
H1, H2

Tropical herbal grass forms 3- to 5-foot clumps of flat green blades. Blooms are seldom seen. All parts of the plant are strongly lemon scented; the pith of the stem base is widely used in Southeast Asian cooking. Plant in full sun; water regularly but don't over-water. Fertilize monthly during summer. Overwinter as a house-plant in a cool, bright spot. Propagate by division.

Cyperus papyrus

Dracaena marginata 'Tricolor'

CYPERUS
Papyrus, umbrella plant
ZONES VARY BY SPECIES

These sedges are valued for striking form and silhouette. Umbrella plant (*C. alternifolius:* zones 8, 9, 12–31; H1, H2) has narrow, firm, spreading leaves arranged like ribs of an umbrella at the tops of 2- to 4-foot stems. Blooms are dry, greenish brown clusters. Grows in or out of water and can be weedy. Dwarf form is 'Gracilis'. Papyrus (*C. papyrus:* zones 16, 17, 23–28; H1, H2) has graceful dark green stems 6 to 10 feet tall, topped with clusters of green threadlike leaves. Plant in full sun and protect from strong wind. Feed monthly. Put in a container and overwinter as a houseplant in standing water.

DATURA
Thorn apple, angel's trumpet
ALL ZONES

Similar in looks and growing needs to *Brugmansia,* to which it is closely related, but there are some important differences. The plants grow quickly from seed to resemble sprawling shrubs 3 to 4 feet tall and wide. They bloom constantly from early summer to frost. Large, fragrant blooms are upright or at right angles to the stem, and the spine-covered seed-pods are the size and shape of eggs. They self-sow but are not weedy, though related to jimson weed. Do not do well in containers unless containers are very large. All parts of the plant are poisonous if ingested.

Datura metel 'Black'

DRACAENA
ZONES VARY BY SPECIES

These evergreen shrubs grow to 2 to 14 feet and come with many different foliage patterns of greens and yellows. Dragon tree (*D. draco:* zones 16, 17, 21–27; H1, H2) has a stout trunk and spreading branches topped with clusters of sword-shaped leaves. Corn plant (*D. fragrans:* zones 21, 23–25, 27; H1, H2) has heavy, ribbonlike blue green leaves 3 feet long, some with yellow stripes. Very popular *D. marginata* (zones 21, 23–25, 27; H1, H2) is slender and erect with gray stems topped by crowns of narrow leathery leaves; some cultivars have red stripes and red foliage. Flowers may be fragrant but not showy. Plant grows in full shade to sun if acclimated. Propagate by cuttings or air layers. Overwinter as a choice houseplant in a bright window.

Eucharis × grandiflora

Duranta erecta

DURANTA erecta
Sky flower, golden dewdrop, pigeon berry
ZONES 13, 16, 17, 21–27; H1, H2

These fast-growing shrubs have small leaves and clusters of lavender blue or white flowers followed by golden berries the size of cherries. There are some variegated cultivars. Can grow to 14 feet in warm climates; stays closer to 3 to 6 feet in cooler climes. Can be pruned as standards or topiaries. Blooms start while plants are still small. Yellow swallowtail butterflies come for nectar. Set out plant in full sun

and feed monthly to encourage new growth and flowers. If taken inside for winter, plant will bloom with enough bright light. Can be forced into dormancy by pruning back to 6 inches and placing in a cool, dark place; or take cuttings.

EUCALYPTUS
ZONES 5, 6, 8–24; H1, H2

Of the many eucalyptus species, a must-have for many gardeners is the silver dollar tree *(E. cinerea),* with its aromatic round silvery blue leaves and stems. It grows 6 to 8 feet tall in a season. Train a central leader branch or the plant will sprawl. Because of shallow roots, it may need staking. Give it full sun and well-drained, moist soil. Feed monthly. Prune often to encourage bright rounded juvenile foliage, popular with florists. If you dry cut foliage, it will last for years. Plants grow quickly from seeds; cuttings are very difficult. Can be used as a perennial in borderline zones; otherwise, force dormancy by cutting back and storing in a cool, dark place.

EUCHARIS × grandiflora
Eucharist lily, Amazon lily
ZONES 25, 26; H1, H2

These shade-loving perennials grow in acid soil and have glossy dark green, hostalike leaves 2 feet long. They bloom in flushes as often as four times a year with lightly lemon-scented, nodding clusters of white, orchidlike flowers that are often used in bridal bouquets. Mature bulbs bear as many as 20 flowering stems a year. Plant in light to dense shade, as sun will burn the leaves. For best bloom, fertilize monthly during active growth. Keep soil moist before and during bloom; let it dry out some for a month after each floral flush so that the plant can rest. Then water again and repeat the cycle. Overwinter as a houseplant; may bloom in winter. Or allow bulbs to dry and go dormant; store like dahlias. Repot and divide bulbs every few years.

Eucalyptus cinerea

Davallia trichomanoides

EUPHORBIA
ZONES VARY BY SPECIES

This genus includes 1,200 very different-looking plants with one thing in common: small flowers surrounded by often showy bracts. The leafy tropical Caribbean copper plant (*E. cotinifolia:* deciduous in zone 23; evergreen in zones 24–27, H1, H2) has a multistemmed trunk with long-stalked wine red leaves 4 inches long and inconspicuous flowers. It can grow 3 feet or more in a season. The old-fashioned snow-on-the-mountain (*E. marginata:* all zones as annual) grows to 2 feet tall; leaves are light green and white. *E. wallichii* (zones 3b–9, 14–16, 18, 28, 31, 33) blooms in early summer. Succulent types include crown of thorns (*E. milii:* zones 13, 21–27; H1, H2), which grows to 4 feet or more, with showy bright coral to red or yellow bracts. Milkbush (*E. tirucalli*: zones 13, 23–25, 27; H1, H2) has pencil-thick, mostly bare succulent branches and is grown for its striking pattern of silhouette and shadow. Plant all species in sun. Plants are drought tolerant; leafy types will take more water and richer soil but should still be watered sparingly and fed only once or twice a year. They make great houseplants on a sunny windowsill. Sap can burn skin or cause a rash.

FERNS
ZONES VARY BY GENUS

Perennial plants grown for lovely and interesting foliage, ferns vary from ground covers to trees up to 50 feet tall. They grow in all parts of the world; some are cold hardy, others tropical. Most are forest plants, but some grow in fields, in deserts, and high in the mountains. The most popular for tropical gardens are *Adiantum, Asplenium, Cyrtomium falcatum, Davallia, Dicksonia, Nephrolepis, Osmunda, Polypodium, Pteris, Rumohra,* and *Thelypteris*; most of these genera include both hardy and tropical or subtropical species.

This ancient form of plant life doesn't flower, reproducing by spores that form directly on the fronds. Some ferns go dormant in the winter; others are evergreen. Most have finely cut green foliage. Some have broad leaves; others have subtle colors, dark brown fertile fronds, or lime green foliage. You'll find ferns with silvery markings or with a touch of red or bluish green in both new growth and fertile fronds.

Most like moist, woodsy, acid soil and shade. Give them plenty of water, and feed tropical varieties monthly with a plant food high in nitrogen, like blood meal or fish emulsion. Natives growing outdoors don't need much feeding. Prune away dead foliage, but don't cut back hardy outdoor ferns until new growth begins, as old fronds protect growing tips. In winter, tropical varieties are best kept in a greenhouse or other humid place away from heat sources.

Euphorbia wallichii

Ficus microcarpa 'Variegata'

FICUS

ZONES VARY BY SPECIES

This genus varies from creeping fig *(F. pumila)*, a small-leafed evergreen vine, to familiar houseplants—rubber tree *(F. elastica)*, fiddleleaf fig *(F. lyrata)*, and weeping fig *(F. benjamina)*—that grow as shrubs indoors and as trees in the tropics and subtropics. Chinese banyan *(F. microcarpa)* has a weeping form. Most are hardy only in the warmest parts of the country but adapt wherever citrus grows. Ficus grow in shade to sun. Keep soil evenly moist, and feed every 2 weeks during active growth. Start new plants from cuttings or air layers. Bring inside in winter.

FIG

ZONES 4–9, 12–31, WARMER PARTS OF 32; H1, H2

This deciduous shrub or small tree grows with large, palmate leaves of velvety green. In the edible fig *(Ficus carica)*, fruits are borne all along the branches with the flower hidden inside. Figs can reach 15 to 30 feet tall and wide but stay smaller in cooler climates. They do well in containers or can be espaliered against a wall. Figs are easy to start from cuttings and grow in full sun. Prune back severely at planting and lightly in early spring. If nematodes are a problem, mulch heavily with organic matter. Roots are near the surface, so avoid deep cultivation. The first crop comes in early summer on the previous year's wood, the second later in summer on new wood. In cool climates, dormant plants can be tipped and buried for the winter or taken indoors for dormant storage.

Ficus carica

Gardenia augusta

GARDENIA augusta

ZONES 7–9, 12–16, 18–28, AND UP TO 33 WITH PROTECTION; H1, H2

Among the most beloved of fragrant flowers, gardenias grow easily as large shrubs, bearing hundreds of satiny white flowers in spring. In cooler climates, choose a cultivar like 'Fortuniana' for more summer bloom. Gardenias' glossy green foliage is also decorative. Dwarf cultivars are good in mixed containers. 'Radicans Variegata' grows only 2 feet tall with variegated foliage. Cultivars 'Chuck Hayes' and 'Kleim's Hardy' survive outdoors with protection down to 0°F/−18°C.

Gardenias need evenly moist acid soil, partial shade to full sun (in cooler climates), and frequent feeding with a fertilizer for acid-loving plants. They like bright light and high humidity, and they are prone to drop their leaves and buds if exposed to drafts or changes of temperature—all of which makes them difficult houseplants. Some people have had indoor success by keeping pots in saucers of water. Otherwise, buy an improved variety in late spring and enjoy it all summer.

GRAPTOPHYLLUM pictum
Caricature plant

ZONE 25, H2; MARGINAL IN
26, H1

The exotic foliage of this shrub
is variegated down its bright
midrib with irregular bands or
splotches of many metallic colors
and shapes. Stems are also colorful.
Flowers are showy short spires of
bright red. Shrubs grow quickly
to 5 feet in warm climates, 2 to
3 feet in a summer anywhere.
Full sun, rich soil, and frequent
watering, feeding, and pinching
will result in much bright new
growth. It's also an easy, though
less common, houseplant. If the
windowsills are full, cut it back
for dormant storage.

Graptophyllum pictum 'Waimea'

Gynura aurantiaca

GYNURA aurantiaca
Purple passion vine, velvet plant

ZONES 25; H2

Not a true vine, this perennial
can get 2 to 3 feet tall in a single
season, but usually it's used as
a sprawling ground cover or a
cascading plant in a pot. The
plant's drawing card is its velvety
green leaves covered with dense,
sun-catching purple hairs. 'Purple
Passion' is a trailing form; *G. bicolor* has large, coarse leaves with
scalloped edges and less intense
color. Most people remove buds;
the yellow or orange flowers tend
to offset the plant's elegant
appearance and also have an odor
many find offensive. Plant in partial to full sun; bright light gives
bright foliage. Keep evenly moist
during active growth, and feed
every 2 weeks with liquid fertilizer. Pinch growing tips often to
prevent legginess. The plant starts
easily from cuttings and over-
winters well as a houseplant.

Helichrysum petiolare 'Limelight'

HELICHRYSUM petiolare
Licorice plant

ZONES 16, 17, 22–24; H1

Inch-long woolly silver or
chartreuse leaves densely cover
trailing stems up to 4 feet long,
sprawl over pot edges, and root
where they touch the ground.
Licorice plant is related to the
curry plant *(H. italicum),* an herb,
and also to the annual straw-
flower *(H. bracteatum).* Among its
varieties are 'Limelight', with
light chartreuse leaves; 'Licorice
Splash', variegated in yellow
and green; and 'Variegatum', with
green leaves edged in white.
Common name aside, this plant
is not in the same family as
licorice, but its fleeting aroma
gives it the name. The foliage of
this fine ornamental withstands
wet, hot summers and light
freezes. With its constant color,
it's also an excellent garden
accent. Take cuttings to overwinter, or treat it as an annual.

105

JATROPHA

ZONES 25, H2; MARGINAL IN 26, H1

Most shrubs, such as peregrina (*J. integerrima*), have bright red five-petaled flowers all summer in irregular clusters atop rich dark green foliage. Cotton-leafed jatropha (*J. gossypifolia*) has inconspicuous flowers and large reddish green foliage. Shrubs grow up to 10 feet high in warmest areas (3 to 4 feet a year) and do well in containers. Give them full sun in cooler climates, sun to light shade in warmer ones, and let soil dry slightly between soakings. Feed monthly in summer. Prune to desired size or form; avoid skin-irritating sap. Overwinter in a greenhouse or as a dormant plant. Cuttings root easily. Shrub also grows quickly from seed, though it may not bloom the first year.

Jatropha integerrima

Justicia brandegeeana

JUSTICIA

ZONES VARY BY SPECIES

Exotic flowers of shrimp plant (*J. brandegeeana*: zones 12, 13, 15–17, 21–27; H1, H2) resemble their namesake. Plant blooms from spring to fall with small white flowers and long-lasting bracts of lime green or russet red against apple green leaves. Grows to 4 feet in partial shade to sun. Yellow shrimp plant (*Pachystachys lutea*: zones 25, H2; marginal in 26, H1) has very similar but stiffer flowers and does best in full shade. Brazilian plume flower (*J. carnea*: zones 8, 9, 13–27; H1, H2) has larger, dark green leaves and dense clusters of pink, yellow, white, or crimson tubular flowers from midsummer to winter. Grow in partial shade to sun. It tolerates dry soil but does best when moist. Prune shrimp plant anytime, Brazilian plume flower soon after flowering. Feed monthly. Overwinter as houseplants or let go dormant. Cuttings root easily.

LANTANA

ZONES 8–10, 12–30; H1, H2

This fast-growing, drought-resistant tropical with its pungent foliage and abundant bright flowers has long been used as an annual in colder climates, a shrub in warmer ones. It's valued for its profuse show of color—every month of the year in frost-free areas. Of the two best-known nursery species, *L. camara* grows up to 6 feet tall and wide with clusters of yellow, orange, or red flowers followed by berries that are poisonous to people but not birds. The shorter *L. montevidensis* makes a good ground cover and is useful for hanging

Lantana camara 'New Gold'

baskets. It has rosy lilac or white flowers and less fruit. All lantanas will attract butterflies. Lantana needs full sun. Feed weekly for best bloom, and cut back to keep it in bounds or from getting leggy. It's highly susceptible to whitefly as a houseplant, so better to overwinter it as a dormant plant or treat it as an annual.

Mandevilla × amoena 'Alice du Pont'

MANDEVILLA
ZONES VARY BY SPECIES

Known for its showy flowers, this genus includes plants formerly called *Dipladenia*. These sprawling evergreen shrubs or tropical vines bloom nonstop from late spring until frost, all year in the tropics. They're root hardy where frosts are mild. *M. × amoena* 'Alice du Pont' (zones 25, 26; H1, H2) twines to 15 feet with as many as 12 deep pink, almost iridescent 4-inch-wide blooms in each cluster. Chilean jasmine (*M. laxa:* zones 4–9, 14–24, 28, 29, 31; H1) grows to more than 15 feet. The plant's leaves are dark green and leathery; the summer flowers are clusters of white with yellow throats. The flower's powerful perfume is similar to that of a gardenia.

Mandevilla needs sturdy support to climb, some tying to start, full sun, and enriched soil with plenty of organic matter. It's a fast grower, especially with frequent watering and feeding, but also tolerates drought and some salt. Smaller forms make good houseplants; they will even bloom in winter with enough light. Larger plants can be cut back and put into dormant storage. Pots should be kept slightly damp, with temperatures from 35 to 40°F/2 to 4°C. Propagate by stem cuttings in spring or summer.

Melianthus major

MELIANTHUS major
Honey bush
ZONES 8, 9, 12–28; H1, H2

With fantastic, unique foliage of bluish green, this subtropical grows 2 to 3 feet a year and can get up to 12 feet tall but is easily kept shorter. Foot-long leaves are divided into strongly toothed leaflets. Plant sprawls naturally or can be staked. Either way, it makes a striking architectural silhouette. It blooms in late winter or early spring with 2-foot spikes of brownish red flowers that hummingbirds love. Plant in full sun or part shade in sandy, moist soil. Feed monthly during active growing season. Cut back as needed, even to a few inches. Overwinter in a cool greenhouse or in dormant storage.

Musa × paradisiaca

MUSA
Banana

ZONES VARY BY SPECIES

With their spectacularly long, broad leaves that rustle in the wind and resound in the rain, bananas capture attention in a tropical garden. They usually grow, bloom, and bear fruit only in warm climates, but these fast-growing perennials that can reach tree height in a single season also make handsome ornamentals in cooler areas. There are many smaller, more cold-hardy species and varieties, some with decorative variegated leaves.

One of the most popular bananas to grow is the Abyssinian banana (*Ensete ventricosum:* zones 13, 15–24; H1, H2). The 'Maurelii' cultivar of this African native, grown for its lush, attractive foliage, has dark red leafstalks and huge leaves tinged with red. The striking plant makes a strong architectural focal point in a garden. It doesn't bloom for four or five years, and then it has only inconspicuous flowers and no fruit.

Once bananas bloom and bear fruit, cut down the stalk; in warm climates, for better fruit, also cut down all but four of the suckers that have formed a clump. Leaving trunks of varying heights will produce more continuous fruit.

Mulch these heavy feeders deeply, and give them full sun for best growth; shelter plants from high wind. Provide plenty of water and frequent fertilizer. Cut off damaged leaves in summer; in winter, wait to cut back damaged foliage until all danger of frost is past. Then cut from the top until you find traces of green growth. Bananas always look bad in winter, and the stem, foliage, and buds die when temperatures drop below freezing for a few hours, but the plants will usually come back from the roots. In cold climates, take bananas in containers indoors as houseplants, or overwinter as dormant plants. For cold-hardy, in-ground types, wrap the tops of plants after frost blackens the leaves, and mulch roots heavily. Banana sap will permanently stain fabric, so wear old clothes when harvesting or pruning.

Cold-Hardy Bananas

When grown in well-drained and heavily mulched soil, some cold-hardy banana cultivars survive in the ground in warm microclimates in southern Ohio, including a new cultivar, *Musa acuminata* 'Rajapuri'. *M. × paradisiaca* 'Mysore' is also hardy, surviving down to −2°F/−19°C. Neither of these, however, will live through the mild, wet winters of the Pacific Northwest. Another reliable variety is Japanese banana *(M. basjoo),* which can survive temperatures as low as −14°F/−26°C with a 1- to 2-foot covering of leaves. It bears ornamental flower clusters and fruit after the plant has produced 30 to 35 leaves. Ornamental Chinese yellow banana *(M. lasiocarpa)* grows in dense short clumps 4 to 6 feet tall and wide with yellow flowers that open like artichokes. It needs more heat to thrive than *M. basjoo.*

Within a few years, cold-hardy bananas probably will bear fruit from in-ground plants throughout the country. In most tropical gardens, the fruit is not as important as the foliage and the flowers are just a bonus, but some gardeners will soon get all three.

Phalaenopsis

ORCHIDS

**ZONES VARY BY SPECIES
AND TYPE**

The orchid family is probably the largest in the plant kingdom, with thousands of genera, species, and hybrids. Some are easy to grow; others are more difficult. The easy ones include many sizes and colors of the large corsage-type orchids *(Cattleya);* the spidery *Brassavola* and *Encyclia;* the smaller, waxy corsage types *(Cymbidium);* the highly variable *Dendrobium;* lady's slipper *(Paphiopedilum);* and moth orchids *(Phalaenopsis).* A few have wonderfully fragrant blooms, but most have no scent.

Each orchid requires a slightly different combination of growing conditions. Most are epiphytes—growing in trees in their native lands—that do best in orchid mix or bare-rooted in a basket of moss. A few grow in the ground. Some orchids require little care, hanging in a tree until they bloom and gracing the garden for the length of the blooming season. Experiment with different types until you find your favorites. It's a good idea to buy orchids in bloom; catalog photos can be deceiving. Orchids will not survive a freeze, so take them indoors until the weather warms. Inside, give them bright light and mist often to provide the required humidity.

ORTHOSIPHON
stamenis
Cat whiskers
**ZONES 25, H2;
MARGINAL IN 26, H1**

This perennial is an exotic member of the mint family. Its white or pale lavender feathery spires bloom in continuous flushes throughout the warm weather. The flower's long stamens extend up to 2 inches beyond the bloom. As plants eventually get woody, taking new cuttings and treating them as annuals or short-lived perennials results in the best bloom. A single plant quickly grows 3 to 4 feet tall and twice as wide. Plants bloom best in full sun but do well in partial shade. They are drought tolerant, but you should water before feeding. Deadhead and pinch to keep plants compact and encourage blooming. Cuttings root easily. In cooler climates, plants can be taken inside, where they will flourish in bright natural light. Or plants can be stored dormant in a cool, dark place until spring.

Orthosiphon stamenis

OSTEOSPERMUM
African daisy

ALL ZONES AS ANNUAL; ZONES 8, 9, 12–24 AS PERENNIAL

Profuse daisylike flowers open in sunlight with ray petals in shades of pink, yellow, lavender, purple, or white, often with dark centers and bronze undersides that are charming when the flowers fold at dusk. Plant is sometimes sold as *Dimorphotheca.* Both mounding and trailing types bloom when nights are cool (to 30 to 40°F/–1 to 4°C), thereby extending the garden's blooming season from spring to fall. Mass beneath summer bloomers that do well in hot, dry conditions. Feed sparingly, or they produce foliage rather than flowers. Buy as an annual, or overwinter with cuttings or seeds; not a good houseplant.

Osteospermum

PALMS

ZONES VARY BY SPECIES

Palms offer promises of warmth and sunshine and give any garden or landscape fascinating silhouettes. Shallow rooted, palms are easy to move, even when large. Most palms are fairly to extremely salt tolerant, making them part of beach scenes throughout the world. Palms usually have fan- or feather-shaped leaves; as they grow, the trees shed old leaves. Some palms have single, tall trunks, and other kinds are smaller with multiple trunks. Bees love the thousands of flowers these trees bear. Fruits are usually nut- or berry-size; coconut is the largest edible fruit of the palms. Palms are fairly easy to grow in tropical or subtropical climes, but a few varieties are surprisingly hardy.

Most palms prefer shade, making them good patio plants when small. Many do well in full sun once they mature. Palms grow rapidly in warm climates. The ones that stay below 10 feet are easy to tend; once they get taller, cleaning up dead leaves and fronds, as well as fallen fruit, can be a problem. Palm fronds are best removed with a palm saw while they are turning yellow; brown fronds are harder to cut.

Palms adapt well to containers and make good houseplants. When they get larger and more

Bismarkia nobilis

top-heavy, protect them from wind, and weight containers with heavy sand or anchor them with metal rods through the drainage holes. Water palms in containers well two or three times a week. Potting soils should be light and porous, or even a mixture of sand and humus. Mature in-ground palms may be drought tolerant but prefer moist, not soggy, soil. Once temperatures are above 60°F/16°C, feed them often. Spray frequently with water to provide some humidity, wash off foliage, and dislodge any insects. To overwinter hardy palms in the ground, wrap with Christmas tree lights to provide a few degrees of frost protection; wrap the tops for more. It's important to protect the palm's crown; damage in the crown is usually fatal.

Choosing the right palm for your garden can seem overwhelming, but don't despair. You can always find just the right palm for any location.

Small to medium-size palms for sheltered areas in frost-free gardens include *Archontophoenix*, *Caryota*, *Chamaedorea*, *Chamaerops*, *Chrysalidocarpus*, and *Howea*.

If you need small to medium-size palms for areas with occasional frosts, look for *Acoelorrhaphe*, *Brahea armata*, *Butia*, *Chamaedorea*, *Chamaerops*, *Livistona*, *Neodypsis*, *Phoenix roebelenii*, *Ptychosperma macarthuri*, and *Trachycarpus*.

The hardiest palms, which will endure temperatures significantly below freezing, are *Brahea armata*, *Chamaerops*, *Jubaea*, *Livistona*, *Phoenix canariensis*, *P. dactylifera*, *P. loureiri*, *Rhapidophyllum hystrix*, *Rhapis*, *Sabal mexicana*, *S. minor*, *S. palmetto*, *Syagrus romanzoffianum*, *Trachycarpus*, and *Washingtonia*.

Frost becomes more damaging to palms as it extends its stay and is repeated. Light frosts for half an hour may leave no damage, but the same frost during a period of 4 hours may damage some palms and kill others. Hardiness is also a matter of size: larger plants may pass through severe frosts unharmed while smaller ones perish.

In hot dry climates, look for *Bismarkia*, *Butia*, *Chamaerops*, *Livistona chinensis*, *L. mariae*, *Phoenix canariensis*, *P. dactylifera*, *P. loureiri*, *P. sylvestris*, *Sabal mexicana*, *S. minor*, and *Washingtonia*. Most also do well in the humid and warm climates of Southern California.

Good choices for growing under lattice or overhangs are *Caryota mitis*, *C. ochlandra*, *C. urens*, *Chamaedorea*, *Howea*, *Livistona* (when young), *Phoenix reclinata* (when young), *P. roebelenii*, and *Rhapis*. Indoor palms should occasionally be brought outdoors into mild light.

Young palms, especially slow growers such as *Livistona chinensis* and *Chamaerops*, are effective as plantings under tall trees. They'll stay low for five to ten years. When they get too tall, move to where you need height.

Thanks to their stateliness and spectacular leaves, palms are good subjects for night lighting. Backlight them, light from below, or direct lights to silhouette them against a wall.

Cold-Hardy Palms

While few of these palms become large trees in colder climates, that's actually an advantage. The very hardiest species are marked with average low temperatures the roots have been known to survive. Heavy mulching helps, as does trunk and top wrapping. Most will lose leaves at higher temperatures but will put out new leaves the next summer if the bud is not harmed. Clump palms and fan palms tend to be hardier, and that hardiness increases as trees mature.

Some palms will resemble perennials in colder climates. Don't be surprised if these die back to the ground in cold winters but regrow as clump palms from the roots when weather warms in spring. Mulch helps protect roots.

PALMS TO GROW AS PERENNIALS
Chamaedorea radicalis (dwarf bamboo palm) 0°F/–18°C
Livistona chinensis (Chinese fountain palm) 20 to 23°F/–7 to –5°C
Phoenix roebelenii (pygmy date palm) 0°F/–18°C

TREES
Butia capitata (pindo palm) Root hardy to 0°F/–18°C
Chamaerops humilis (Mediterranean fan palm) Root hardy to 3°F/–16°C
Sabal palmetto (cabbage palm) 0°F/–18°C
Trachycarpus fortunei (windmill palm) –12°F/–24°C
Washingtonia species (fan palm) –1°F/–18°C

SHRUBS
Nannorrhops ritchiana (Mazari palm) 0°F/–18°C
Rhapidophyllum hystrix (needle palm) –14°F/–26°C
Sabal species (palmettos) –5°F/–21°C
Serenoa repens (saw palmetto) 0°F/–18°C
Trachycarpus fortunei (Chinese windmill palm) –12°F/–24°C
Trithrinax campestris (blue needle palm) –12°F/–24°C

Passiflora caerulea

PASSIFLORA
Passion vine
ZONES VARY BY SPECIES

Birds are attracted to the exquisite 1- to 6-inch-wide flowers, as in *P. caerulea; P. coccinea* has scarlet flowers with recurved petals (zones 5–9, 12–24; H1, H2). Many produce edible fruit. Let the vigorous vine climb a trellis or tree; can be invasive in warm climates. Does best in full sun but will take partial shade. Let soil dry between waterings. Feed every 2 weeks with bloom-booster fertilizer. Prune annually. Over-winter with stem cuttings or as a dormant container plant.

PENNISETUM
Fountain grass
ZONES VARY BY SPECIES

Graceful, clump-forming orna-mental grasses (zones 8–24, 26, 27, 28 [warmer parts]; H1, H2), *P. setaceum* and feathertop

(*P. villosum*) are often grown as annuals in colder climates. *P. setaceum* has medium green foliage with coppery pink or purplish plumes. 'Rubrum' has burgundy leaves and does not set seed. 'Burgundy Giant' gets 7 feet tall. Feathertop has thin, light green leaves and 2-inch-long white plumes. All grasses need full sun and like regular watering but are very drought tolerant. If they don't die back in winter, they can be pruned to the ground in early spring to remove dead foliage. Feed monthly in summer. Some species seed freely and may be invasive where perennial. Can overwinter dormant in a basement or garage.

Pennisetum setaceum 'Rubrum'

Pentas lanceolata

PENTAS lanceolata
Star clusters
ZONES 23, 24; H1, H2;
ALL ZONES AS ANNUAL

This prince among plants will bloom virtually every warm day of the year with bright 2-inch clusters of small star-shaped flowers. A perennial where frost does not set it back, the plant can grow 4 to 5 feet tall. Foliage is dark green, and flowers are red, white, or shades of pink to purple; a dwarf variety has bluish blooms. Plants always look neat. Pentas—particularly the red pentas—are a favorite with butterflies. They are also good as cut flowers. Give them full sun or partial shade and let soil dry between waterings. Feed every other week during the summer. Prune plants to keep compact. Cuttings root easily, but it's best to buy pentas as annuals in cold climates; they draw whiteflies indoors.

PHORMIUM

ZONES 7–9, 14–28; H1, H2;
ROOT HARDY IN 5, 6

This striking plant offers both dramatic shape and bold color. A cousin of the agave, it grows with a central rosette of erect, sword-shaped leaves up to 10 feet tall, 1 to 4 feet the first season. Plants are grown for their brightly colored foliage, from green and bronze to red and gold. Flowers, which are dull red to reddish orange, are rare beyond the tropics. The rugged plant adapts well to containers; thrives in sun to light shade; and prefers cool, dry climates. Feed once or twice in summer. Increase by seed or division; it takes two to three years to get specimen plants. Overwinter as a houseplant in a cool, bright spot, or put in dormant storage. If well mulched, it may be root hardy to 0°F/−18°C.

Plumeria obtusa

Phormium

PLUMERIA
Frangipani

ZONES VARY BY SPECIES

The pride of Hawaii, this flower decorates leis, enchanting visitors with its marvelous fragrance and simple waxy beauty. The plant blooms in warm weather with clusters of colorful flowers in white, yellow, or shades of pink and red. Shrubs or small trees are open in habit, deciduous, and tender to frost, cold, and wet soil. Dwarf varieties grow only a few feet tall. All plants can be pruned to keep them from becoming leggy. Singapore plumeria *(P. obtusa)* and white frangipani *(P. alba)* grow in zones 24, 25, and H2. *P. rubra* grows in zones 12, 13, 19, 21–25, 27; H1, H2. All need full sun. Let soil dry out after watering; mature plants are drought tolerant. Feed every 2 weeks. Frangipani does well in containers. It goes dormant naturally; bring inside before frost and store in a cool place. Plant roots easily from cuttings.

Ricinus communis

RICINUS communis
Castor bean
ZONES 24, 25; H1, H2

Gardeners all over the country grow this as a summer annual. The fast grower (10 feet or more in a season) has 2-foot-wide leaves and unusual burrlike seed capsules that give any garden a tropical feel. Varieties include 'Carmencita', with brilliant red flower buds and seedpods, and reddish burgundy to brown leaves and stems; 'Carmencita Pink', with pink fruit; and 'Zanzibarensis', with huge, white-veined bright green leaves. Castor bean's flowers are inconspicuous; spires of seeds are long lasting. The plant is an herb, the source of castor oil. Although a perennial in warm regions, it's usually considered an annual. Save seeds and start over each spring; self-sows in mild climates. Plant it in full sun; provide water and fertilizer as needed. It's fairly tolerant of both drought and salt.

Warning

The attractive seeds of castor bean are so poisonous if ingested that even one can be deadly. Grow these plants only after your children have passed the stage of putting things in their mouths; also warn visitors with small children. Handling foliage and seeds can also irritate the skin of those allergic to ricin.

SANCHEZIA speciosa
ZONES 25, H2; MARGINAL IN 26, H1

Few shrubs have such bright, variegated foliage. Foot-long leaves start out green with white or yellow veins and turn yellow in bright sun. Plants are nipped by a hint of frost but come back reliably in zone 26. Plants will bloom in shade, which provides more protection from frost. Flowers are small and yellow. Stems of 6 to 12 odd-shaped red bracts last for a long time. Feed every 2 weeks. Pinch or prune to shape and encourage colorful new growth. Overwinter as a houseplant if you can give it high humidity; a greenhouse works better. Container-grown plants can also go into dormant storage.

Sanchezia speciosa

Sansevieria trifasciata 'Laurentii'

SANSEVIERIA trifasciata
Snake plant

ZONES 13, 23–25; H1, H2

This hard-to-kill houseplant makes a strong vertical accent in a garden. It's appreciated for its thick, rigidly upright, patterned leaves. Scores of other species and varieties can be found in succulent catalogs. The plant bears erect narrow clusters of fragrant, greenish white flowers in Hawaii but seldom blooms elsewhere; however, mature plants may surprise you after a summer outdoors. Watch for long spires, and bring container plants indoors or onto a patio to enjoy the blooms' heady perfume at night. A bloom-booster fertilizer every 2 weeks in the summer increases chances of blooming. Plant in shade or acclimate to full sun. Plants enjoy spending the winter indoors.

SENNA
ZONES VARY BY SPECIES

These shrubs or small trees can grow to 10 feet or more in the tropics, even climbing 4 to 8 feet a year if not pinched back. Start seeds of the candle bush (*S. alata*: zones 25, 26; H1, H2) indoors in February, and plants will bloom in late summer and fall with spires of bright yellow flowers on long, naked stems with tight green buds at the tips. Seedpods look like furry, flat beans and sprout easily. Even if it doesn't bloom, candle bush makes a fine architectural plant, with long, compound leaves. All sennas need full sun. Plants may be covered with blankets of yellow flowers for weeks at a time. *S. artemisioides* (zones 8, 9, 12–16, 18–23) blooms in the desert. Where the ground doesn't freeze, candle bush may die back in winter and come back from roots in spring. Sennas also can be grown as annuals.

Senna artemisioides

Solanum jasminoides

SOLANUM
ZONES VARY BY SPECIES

In addition to eggplant and potato, this genus includes other decorative vines and shrubs as well as perennial cousins. Fruit is poisonous if ingested (though it doesn't seem to hurt birds, who are drawn to it); berries can be tempting to children. Potato vine (*S. jasminoides:* zones 8, 9, 12–27; H1, H2) twines to 30 feet with purple-tinged leaves and clusters of flowers that are white or white tinged with blue. Jerusalem cherry (*S. pseudocapsicum*) is a shrub in zones 23–27, H1, and H2, and an annual or indoor/outdoor plant anywhere. Flowers are small and white like pepper blossoms. Birds enjoy the decorative fruit. Grow in full sun (light shade in warm climates). Plants are not fussy eaters but are more colorful if fed every 2 weeks. Overwinter as houseplants or in dormant storage.

STRELITZIA reginae
Bird of paradise
ZONES 22–25, 26 (SOUTHERN PART), 27, H1, H2; MARGINAL IN 9, 12–21

Perhaps the most flamboyant of flowers, these look like blue-and-orange birds about to take flight. Flowers and bracts are long lasting. Plant grows 3 to 5 feet tall with a basal clump of long-stalked, blue green, paddle-shaped leaves and does well in containers. Flowers bloom intermittently through the year, mostly in the cool season. Large, crowded clumps or pot-bound plants bloom best in full sun; in hot climates, leaves stay nicer in partial shade. Give plants rich soil and let it dry between waterings. Feed monthly during active growth. Even the foliage is a fine addition to the tropical garden, which is good since plants may not bloom until they are five years old. Overwinter as a houseplant, keeping soil fairly dry. Resume regular watering and feeding in spring.

Strelitzia reginae

Strobilanthes dyeranus

STROBILANTHES dyeranus
Persian shield

ZONES 25, H2; MARGINAL IN
26, H1

Only the edges and veins of
Persian shield's leaves are green;
the rest of the foliage is an
iridescent purple, dark in new
growth and turning silver
as it matures. The plant's
dark purple blossoms are
interesting in early spring
but detract from the showy
foliage. Plants grow 2 to 4
feet a season. Prune or
pinch to encourage new
growth (leaves are attractive in bouquets). Provide
partial shade where sum-
mers are hot. These very
thirsty plants will wilt with
too much sun, no matter
how much you water.
Feed every 2 weeks in
summer and mulch ankle-
deep with organic matter.
In warm climates take
cuttings before a frost; in
cool zones overwinter as
a houseplant (leaves may
not shine as brightly
indoors); take new cut-
tings for spring planting.

SUCCULENTS

ZONES VARY BY GENUS

Any plant that stores water in
juicy leaves, stems, or roots to
withstand periodic drought is a
succulent. Many are easy to grow
anywhere as houseplants and in
warm climates as landscape plants.
They are particularly useful in
containers. *Agave, Aloe,* bromeliads, *Euphorbia,* and *Sansevieria*
are listed in this encyclopedia.
Others of merit include the
many species and varieties of
Crassula, Echeveria, Epiphyllum,
Kalanchoe, Rhipsalidopsis,
Schlumbergera, Sedum, and *Yucca.*

Some have fantastic foliage and
architectural splendor; some,
long-lasting flowers.

Give all these plants just
enough water to keep them
healthy, plump of leaf, and
attractive. Most take full sun to
partial shade. Feed lightly at the
beginning of the growing season. Larger and later-blooming
kinds may require additional
feeding. Easy to start from cuttings. Combine them carefully
with other types of plants, both
for cultural requirements and
for aesthetic value. Overwinter
as houseplants in cool climates.

Succulents, including spiky agaves and cacti

Thunbergia grandiflora

THUNBERGIA

ZONES VARY BY SPECIES

These fast-growing tropical plants are known for bright, beautiful flowers. Some, like black-eyed Susan vine (*T. alata*), are sold in hanging baskets everywhere. They not only live through winter but can also take over a garden in zones 23–27; H1, H2. Once it's a year old, sky flower (*T. grandiflora:* zones 16, 21–27; H1, H2) has gorgeous curtains of flaring tubular 3-inch flowers in delicate pure blue in summer and fall. Orange clock vine (*T. gregorii*) has bright orange blooms nearly year-round. It's a perennial in zones 21–27, H1, and H2, and a summer annual elsewhere. Other species have blooms of blue, purple, gold, or satiny white. Vines can be started from seeds or cuttings. Planting with seeds may result in color variations. Plants need full sun for best bloom, enriched soil, plenty of water, and regular feeding. In warm climates, prune to control growth. In cold climates, most are treated as annuals and restarted from seeds. Overwinter sky flower in a greenhouse or buy older container plants in spring.

TIBOUCHINA

ZONES 16, 17, 21-27; H1, H2

This 12- to 15-foot shrub, which grows 3 to 8 feet a season, blooms in a blanket of deep purple or pink flowers that can stop traffic. It has large, deeply veined, usually hairy leaves. Princess flower (*T. grandiflora*) has larger leaves and big clusters of brilliant royal purple flowers. Leaves turn bright orange in fall. Give *Tibouchina* full sun and plenty of water, and feed monthly. Mulch well where nematodes are a problem. Overwinter with cuttings or as dormant container plants. Smaller plants make fine houseplants.

Tibouchina grandiflora

Tradescantia virginiana

TRADESCANTIA

ZONES 12–24; H1, H2

Whether indoor houseplants or outside ground cover, these are hardy plants. They have long trailing, jointed succulent stems of colorful foliage and small pink, white, or lavender flowers. Among the species are wandering Jew (*T. fluminensis* and *T. zebrina*), Moses-in-the-cradle (*T. spathacea*), and spiderwort (*T. virginiana*), as well as purple heart (*T. pallida* 'Purpurea') and other cultivars. Plants grow easily in full sun to full shade, in sidewalk cracks, or even in standing water, but they prefer moist soil. In frost-free areas the plants are perennials; they also can overwinter easily as large plants or from cuttings.

ZINGIBERACEAE

ZONES VARY BY SPECIES

Gingers grow to their full height (1 to 8 feet) in one season and offer lush foliage and wonderful flowers for very little effort.

Alpinia (zones 14-29; H1, H2) is root hardy to 15°F/–9°C and grows year-round with fragrant white to pinkish flowers.

Ginger lily (*Hedychium:* zones 8, 9, 14–17, 19–27; H1, H2) has showy flowers. Butterfly lily (*H. coronarium*) is one of several gingers with deliciously fragrant white or pale yellow orchidlike flowers. Other lilies may have brightly colored blooms. Plants grow 2 to 9 feet and go dormant in winter.

True ginger (*Zingiber officinale:* zones 9, 14–28; H1, H2) is used in cooking. Buy roots fresh at a grocery in spring; cut into 1- to 2-inch sections, each with a bud; and plant the sections flat just below the soil surface. Bloom takes a long time, but you can cut off pieces of rhizome as needed for cooking the first summer. Goes dormant in winter. Where soil freezes, dig and store indoors.

Pine cone ginger (*Z. zerumbet:* zones 9, 14–28; H1, H2) has pineconeshaped clusters of bracts you can squeeze for a lanolinlike lotion. Smaller gingers include *Globba,*

with arching sprays of intricate flowers, and *Kaempferia,* which can be used as a ground cover (zones 25, 26; H1, H2). *Curcuma* (zones 14–24; H1, H2) has exotic flowers in white, pink, or rose.

Gingers with narrow leaves do best in part to full sun; those with wide leaves prefer light shade. Pine cone ginger grows well in deep shade to full sun. All need moist, enriched, slightly acidic soil. Use slow-release fertilizer at planting, and feed every 2 weeks with liquid food for best growth and bloom. The evergreens, such as *Alpinia,* make good houseplants.

Globba winitii 'Dancing Ladies'

SUNSET'S GARDEN CLIMATE ZONES

A plant's performance is governed by the total climate: length of growing season, timing and amount of rainfall, winter lows, summer highs, humidity. *Sunset*'s climate zone maps take all these factors into account—unlike the familiar hardiness zone maps devised by the U.S. Department of Agriculture, which divide the U.S. and Canada into zones based strictly on winter lows. The U.S.D.A. maps tell you only where a plant may survive the winter; our climate zone maps let you see where that plant will thrive year-round. Below and on pages 124–125 are brief descriptions of the zones illustrated on the maps on pages 125–127. For more information, consult *Sunset*'s regional garden books.

ZONE 1A. Coldest Mountain and Intermountain Areas in the West

Growing season: mid-June to early Sept. All zone is west of Continental Divide, with mild days, chilly nights. Average lows to −0°F/−18°C, extreme lows to −40°F/−40°C; snow cover (or winter mulch) key to perennials' success.

ZONE 1B. Coldest Eastern Rockies and Plains Climate

Growing season: mid-May to late Sept. All zone is east of Continental Divide, with warm days, warmer nights than 1A. Summer rainfall present, wind a constant. Winter arctic cold fronts create sudden temperature shifts; average lows to 0°F/−18°C, extreme lows to −50°F/−46°C.

ZONE 2A. Cold Mountain and Intermountain Areas

Growing season: mid-May to mid-Sept. Occurs at lower elevation than Zone 1A; summers are mild, winters to 10°F/−12°C (extremes to −30°F/−34°C) with snow. The coldest zone for growing sweet cherries, hardiest apples.

ZONE 2B. Warmer-summer Intermountain Climate

Growing season: mid-May to Oct. Premier fruit- and grain-growing climate with long, warm to hot summers. Winters to 12°F/−11°C (extremes to −20°F/−29°C) with snow.

ZONE 3A. Mild Areas of Mountain and Intermountain Climates

Growing season: May to mid-Oct. Long, dry, warm summers favor a variety of warm-season crops, deciduous fruits, many ornamentals. Occurs at higher elevation the farther south it is found. Winter temperatures drop to 15°F/−9°C with extremes to −18°F/−28°C; snow is possible.

ZONE 3B. Mildest Areas of Intermountain Climates

Growing season: early April to late Oct. Compared with Zone 3A, summers are warmer, winters milder: to 19°F/−7°C with extremes to −15°F/−26°C. Snow is possible. Excellent climate for vegetables, also a wide variety of ornamentals that prefer dry atmosphere.

ZONE 4. Cold-winter Western Washington and British Columbia

Growing season: early May to early Oct. Summers are cool, thanks to ocean influence; chilly winters (19° to −7°F/−7° to −22°C) result from elevation, influence of continental air mass, or both. Coolness, ample rain suit many perennials and bulbs.

ZONE 5. Ocean-influenced Northwest Coast and Puget Sound

Growing season: mid-April to Nov., typically with cool temperatures throughout. Less rain falls here than in Zone 4; winter lows range from 28° to 1°F/−2° to −17°C. This "English garden" climate is ideal for rhododendrons and many rock garden plants.

ZONE 6. Oregon's Willamette Valley

Growing season: mid-Mar. to mid-Nov., with somewhat warmer temperatures than in Zone 5. Ocean influence keeps winter lows about the same as in Zone 5. Climate suits all but tender plants and those needing hot or dry summers.

ZONE 7. Oregon's Rogue River Valley, California's High Foothills

Growing season: May to early Oct. Summers are hot and dry; typical winter lows run from 23° to 9°F/−5° to −13°C. The summer-winter contrast suits plants that need dry, hot summers and moist, only moderately cold winters.

ZONE 8. Cold-air Basins of California's Central Valley

Growing season: mid-Feb. through Nov. This is a valley floor with no maritime influence. Summers are hot; winter lows range from 29° to 13°F/−2° to −11°C. Rain comes in the cooler months, covering just the early part of the growing season.

ZONE 9. Thermal Belts of California's Central Valley

Growing season: late Feb. through Dec. Zone 9 is located in the higher elevations around Zone 8, but its summers are just as hot; its winter lows are slightly higher (temperatures range from 28° to 18°F/−2° to −8°C). Rainfall pattern is the same as in Zone 8.

ZONE 10. High Desert Areas of Arizona, New Mexico, West Texas, Oklahoma Panhandle, and Southwest Kansas

Growing season: April to early Nov. Chilly (even snow-dusted) weather rules from late Nov. through Feb., with lows from 31° to 24°F/−1° to −4°C. Rain comes in summer as well as in the cooler seasons.

ZONE 11. Medium to High Desert of California and Southern Nevada

Growing season: early April to late Oct. Summers are sizzling, with 110 days above 90°F/32°C. Balancing this is a 3½-month winter, with 85 nights below freezing and lows from 11° to 0°F/−12° to −18°C. Scant rainfall comes in winter.

ZONE 12. Arizona's Intermediate Desert

Growing season: mid-Mar. to late Nov., with scorching midsummer heat. Compared with Zone 13, this region has harder frosts; record low is 6°F/−14°C. Rains come in summer and winter.

ZONE 13. Low or Subtropical Desert

Growing season: mid-Feb. through Nov., interrupted by nearly 3 months of incandescent, growth-stopping summer heat. Most frosts are light (record lows run from 19° to 13°F/−7° to −11°C); scant rain comes in summer and winter.

ZONE 14. Inland Northern and Central California with Some Ocean Influence

Growing season: early Mar. to mid-Nov., with rain coming in the remaining months. Periodic intrusions of marine air temper summer heat and winter cold (lows run from 26° to 16°F/−3° to −9°C). Mediterranean-climate plants are at home here.

ZONE 15. Northern and Central California's Chilly-winter Coast-influenced Areas

Growing season: Mar. to Dec. Rain comes from fall through winter. Typical winter lows range from 28° to 21°F/−2° to −6°C. Maritime air influences the zone much of the time, giving it cooler, moister summers than Zone 14.

ZONE 16. Northern and Central California Coast Range Thermal Belts

Growing season: late Feb. to late Nov. With cold air draining to lower elevations, winter lows typically run from 32° to 19°F/0° to −7°C. Like Zone 15, this region is dominated by maritime air, but its winters are milder on average.

ZONE 17. Oceanside Northern and Central California and Southernmost Oregon

Growing season: late Feb. to early Dec. Coolness and fog are hallmarks; summer highs seldom top 75°F/24°C, while winter lows run from 36° to 23°F/2° to −5°C. Heat-loving plants disappoint or dwindle here.

ZONE 18. Hilltops and Valley Floors of Interior Southern California

Growing season: mid-Mar. through late Nov. Summers are hot and dry; rain comes in winter, when lows reach 28° to 10°F/–2° to –12°C. Plants from the Mediterranean and Near Eastern regions thrive here.

ZONE 19. Thermal Belts around Southern California's Interior Valleys

Growing season: early Mar. through Nov. As in Zone 18, rainy winters and hot, dry summers are the norm—but here, winter lows dip only to 27° to 22°F/–3° to –6°C, allowing some tender evergreen plants to grow outdoors with protection.

ZONE 20. Hilltops and Valley Floors of Ocean-influenced Inland Southern California

Growing season: late Mar. to late Nov.—but fairly mild winters (lows of 28° to 23°F/–2° to –5°C) allow gardening through much of the year. Cool and moist maritime influence alternates with hot, dry interior air.

ZONE 21. Thermal Belts around Southern California's Ocean-influenced Interior Valleys

Growing season: early Mar. to early Dec., with same tradeoff of oceanic and interior influence as in Zone 20. During winter rainy season, lows range from 36° to 23°F/2° to –5°C—warmer than Zone 20, since colder air drains to the valleys.

ZONE 22. Colder-winter Parts of Southern California's Coastal Region

Growing season: Mar. to early Dec. Winter lows seldom fall below 28°F/–2°C (records are around 21°F/–6°C), though colder air sinks to this zone from Zone 23. Summers are warm; rain comes in winter. Climate here is largely oceanic.

ZONE 23. Thermal Belts of Southern California's Coastal Region

Growing season: almost year-round (all but first half of Jan.). Rain comes in winter. Reliable ocean influence keeps summers mild (except when hot Santa Ana winds come from inland), frosts negligible; 23°F/–5°C is the record low.

ZONE 24. Marine-dominated Southern California Coast

Growing season: all year, but periodic freezes have dramatic effects (record lows are 33° to 20°F/1° to –7°C). Climate here is oceanic (but warmer than oceanic Zone 17), with cool summers, mild winters. Subtropical plants thrive.

ZONE 25. South Florida and the Keys

Growing season: all year. Add ample year-round rainfall (least in Dec. through Mar.), high humidity, and overall warmth, and you have a near-tropical climate. The Keys are frost-free; winter lows elsewhere run from 40° to 25°F/4° to –4°C.

ZONE 26. Central and Interior Florida

Growing season: early Feb. to late Dec., with typically humid, warm to hot weather. Rain is plentiful all year, heaviest in summer and early fall. Lows range from 15°F/–9°C in the north to 27°F/–3°C in the south; arctic air brings periodic hard freezes.

ZONE 27. Lower Rio Grande Valley

Growing season: early Mar. to mid-Dec. Summers are hot and humid; winter lows only rarely dip below freezing. Many plants from tropical and subtropical Africa and South America are well adapted here.

ZONE 28. Gulf Coast, North Florida, Atlantic Coast to Charleston

Growing season: mid-Mar. to early Dec. Humidity and rainfall are year-round phenomena; summers are hot, winters virtually frostless but subject to periodic invasions by frigid arctic air. Azaleas, camellias, many subtropicals flourish.

ZONE 29. Interior Plains of South Texas

Growing season: mid-Mar. through Nov. Moderate rainfall (to 25" annually) comes year-round. Summers are hot. Winter lows can dip to 26°F/–3°C, with occasional arctic freezes bringing much lower readings.

ZONE 30. Hill Country of Central Texas

Growing season: mid-Mar. through Nov. Zone 30 has higher annual rainfall than Zone 29 (to 35") and lower winter temperatures, normally to around 20°F/–7°C. Seasonal variations favor many fruit crops, perennials.

ZONE 31. Interior Plains of Gulf Coast and Coastal Southeast

Growing season: mid-Mar. to early Nov. In this extensive east-west zone, hot and sticky summers contrast with chilly winters (record low temperatures are 7° to 0°F/–14° to –18°C). There's rain all year (an annual average of 50"), with the least falling in Oct.

ZONE 32. Interior Plains of Mid-Atlantic States; Chesapeake Bay, Southeastern Pennsylvania, Southern New Jersey

Growing season: late Mar. to early Nov. Rain falls year-round (40" to 50" annually); winter lows (moving through the zone from south to north) are 30° to 20°F/–1° to –7°C. Humidity is less oppressive here than in Zone 31.

ZONE 33. North-Central Texas and Oklahoma Eastward to the Appalachian Foothills

Growing season: mid-April through Oct. Warm Gulf Coast air and colder continental/arctic fronts both play a role; their unpredictable interplay results in a wide range in annual rainfall (22" to 52") and winter lows (20° to 0°F/–7° to –18°C). Summers are muggy and warm to hot.

ZONE 34. Lowlands and Coast from Gettysburg to North of Boston

Growing season: late April to late Oct. Ample rainfall and humid summers are the norm. Winters are variable—typically fairly mild (around 20°F/–7°C), but with lows down to –3° to –22°F/–19° to –30°C if arctic air swoops in.

ZONE 35. Ouachita Mountains, Northern Oklahoma and Arkansas, Southern Kansas to North-Central Kentucky and Southern Ohio

Growing season: late April to late Oct. Rain comes in all seasons. Summers can be truly hot and humid. Without arctic fronts, winter lows are around 18°F/–8°C; with them, the coldest weather may bring lows of –20°F/–29°C.

ZONE 36. Appalachian Mountains

Growing season: May to late Oct. Thanks to greater elevation, summers are cooler and less humid, winters colder (0° to –20°F/–18° to –29°C) than in adjacent, lower zones. Rain comes all year (heaviest in spring). Late frosts are common.

ZONE 37. Hudson Valley and Appalachian Plateau

Growing season: May to mid-Oct., with rainfall throughout. Lower in elevation than neighboring Zone 42, with warmer winters: lows are 0° to –5°F/–18° to –21°C, unless arctic air moves in. Summer is warm to hot, humid.

ZONE 38. New England Interior and Lowland Maine

Growing season: May to early Oct. Summers feature reliable rainfall and lack oppressive humidity of lower-elevation, more southerly areas. Winter lows dip to –10° to –20°F/–23° to –29°C, with periodic colder temperatures due to influxes of arctic air.

ZONE 39. Shoreline Regions of the Great Lakes

Growing season: early May to early Oct. Springs and summers are cooler here, autumns milder than in areas farther from the lakes. Southeast lakeshores get the heaviest snowfalls. Lows reach 0° to –10°F/–18° to –23°C.

ZONE 40. Inland Plains of Lake Erie and Lake Ontario

Growing season: mid-May to mid-Sept., with rainy, warm, variably humid weather. The lakes help moderate winter lows; temperatures typically range from –10° to –20°F/–23° to –29°C, with occasional colder readings when arctic fronts rush through.

Sunset's Garden Climate Zones

Climate Zones	⧄	1A	1B	2A	2B	3A	3B	4	5	6	7	8	9	10	11	12	13	14	15	16	17	18	19	20	21

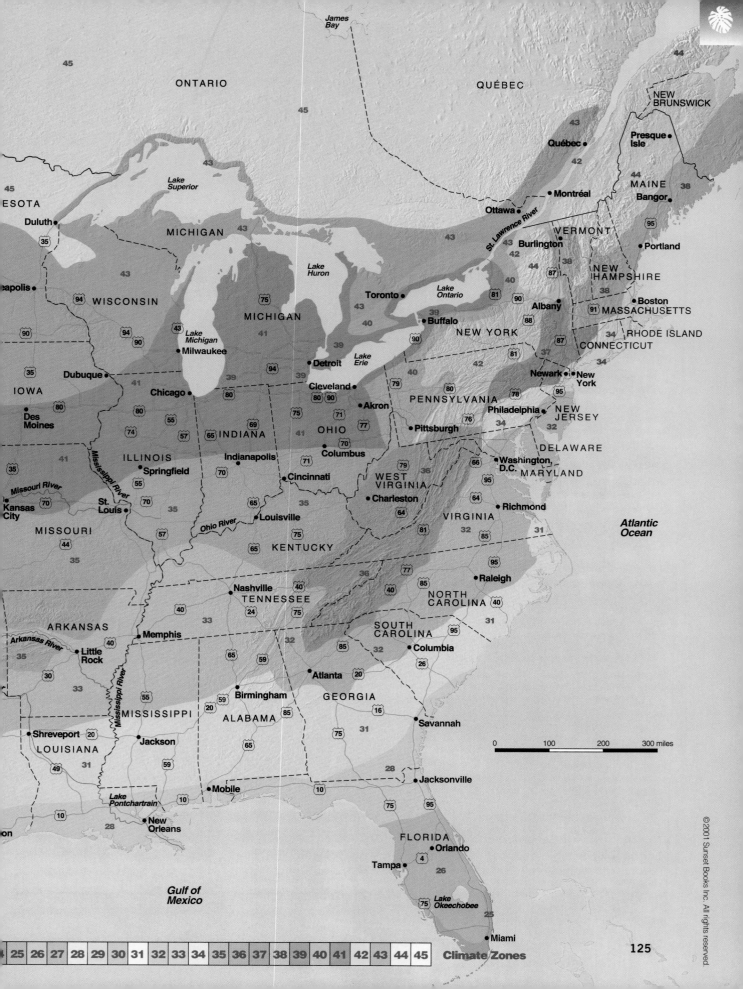

James
Bay

ONTARIO

QUÉBEC

NEW
BRUNSWICK

45

45

45

Lake
Superior

43

Québec

43

Presque
Isle

44

44

38

MAINE

Bangor

ESOTA

Duluth

(35)

43

MICHIGAN

43

Montréal

Ottawa

St. Lawrence River

VERMONT

43

(95)

Portland

eapolis

(94)

WISCONSIN

43

43

Lake
Huron

(75)

43

Burlington

42

44

38

NEW
HAMPSHIRE

38

(87)

(90)

Boston

(90)

(94)

(43)

Lake
Michigan

Milwaukee

MICHIGAN

41

39

Toronto

Lake
Ontario

Buffalo

40

Albany

88

(81)

91

(87)

MASSACHUSETTS

(34)

RHODE ISLAND

(90)

(35)

Dubuque

41

Chicago

(80)

39

Detroit

Lake
Erie

Cleveland

(80)(90)

39

NEW YORK

(90)

40

(79)

42

(81)

37

(87)

CONNECTICUT

(34)

IOWA

(80)

(90)

55

(69)

INDIANA

Akron

(71)

41

OHIO

(77)

PENNSYLVANIA

(80)

(78)

Newark

New
York

(95)

Des
Moines

(74)

(57)

(65)

Indianapolis

(70)

Columbus

(70)

(71)

Cincinnati

39

36

(76)

Pittsburgh

(34)

Philadelphia

NEW
JERSEY

32

DELAWARE

41

(35)

ILLINOIS

Springfield

55

Louisville

(65)

35

WEST
VIRGINIA

Charleston

(79)

66

Washington,
D.C.

MARYLAND

Missouri River

(70)

St.
Louis

(70)

Ohio River

(57)

(75)

KENTUCKY

64

(64)

VIRGINIA

(95)

Richmond

Kansas
City

MISSOURI

(44)

35

(65)

36

(81)

32

(85)

31

Atlantic
Ocean

35

(40)

Nashville

(40)

TENNESSEE

(40)

(24)

(75)

36

(77)

(85)

(40)

Raleigh

NORTH
CAROLINA

(40)

ARKANSAS

33

(95)

Arkansas River

(40)

Memphis

32

31

Little
Rock

(30)

33

(65)

(59)

(85)

32

SOUTH
CAROLINA

(95)

Columbia

(26)

35

(55)

59

Birmingham

Atlanta

(20)

(20)

GEORGIA

(16)

Savannah

Shreveport

(20)

MISSISSIPPI

ALABAMA

(85)

(75)

31

LOUISIANA

(49)

31

Jackson

(65)

(59)

28

Jacksonville

(10)

Mobile

(10)

(75)

(95)

(10)

28

Lake
Pontchartrain

(10)

New
Orleans

FLORIDA

Orlando

(4)

Tampa

26

Gulf of
Mexico

(75)

Lake
Okeechobee

25

Miami

0   100   200   300 miles

| 25 | 26 | 27 | 28 | 29 | 30 | 31 | 32 | 33 | 34 | 35 | 36 | 37 | 38 | 39 | 40 | 41 | 42 | 43 | 44 | 45 | **Climate Zones**

125

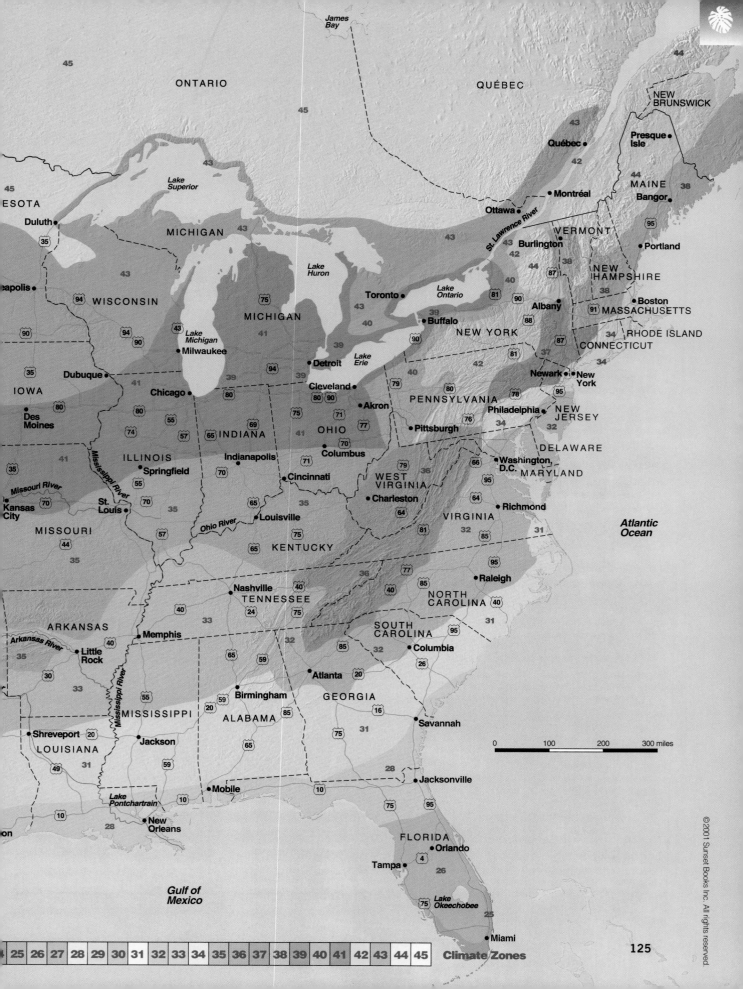

125

© 2001 Sunset Books Inc. All rights reserved.

| 25 | 26 | 27 | 28 | 29 | 30 | 31 | 32 | 33 | 34 | 35 | 36 | 37 | 38 | 39 | 40 | 41 | 42 | 43 | 44 | 45 | **Climate Zones**

ZONE 41. Northeast Kansas and Southeast Nebraska to Northern Illinois and Indiana, Southeast Wisconsin, Michigan, Northern Ohio

Growing season: early May to early Oct. Winter brings average lows of –11° to –20°F/–23° to –29°C. Summers in this zone are hotter and longer west of the Mississippi, cooler and shorter nearer the Great Lakes; summer rainfall increases in the same west-to-east direction.

ZONE 42. Interior Pennsylvania and New York; St. Lawrence Valley

Growing season: late May to late Sept. This zone's elevation gives it colder winters than surrounding zones: lows range from –20° to –40°F/–29° to –40°C, with the colder readings coming in the Canadian portion of the zone. Summers are humid, rainy.

ZONE 43. Upper Mississippi Valley, Upper Michigan, Southern Ontario and Quebec

Growing season: late May to mid-Sept. The climate is humid from spring through early fall; summer rains are usually dependable. Arctic air dominates in winter, with lows typically from –20° to –30°F/–29° to –34°C.

ZONE 44. Mountains of New England and Southeastern Quebec

Growing season: June to mid-Sept. Latitude and elevation give fairly cool, rainy summers, cold winters with lows of –20° to –40°F/–29° to –40°C. Choose short-season, low heat-requirement annuals and vegetables.

ZONE 45. Northern Parts of Minnesota and Wisconsin, Eastern Manitoba through Interior Quebec

Growing season: mid-June through Aug., with rain throughout; rainfall (and humidity) are least in zone's western part, greatest in eastern reaches. Winters are frigid (–30° to –40°F/–34° to –40°C), with snow cover, deeply frozen soil.

ZONE A1. Alaska's Coldest Climate—Fairbanks and the Interior

Growing season: mid-May to early Sept. Summer days are long, mild to warm; permafrost usually recedes below root zone. Winter offers reliable snow cover. Season extenders include planting in south and west exposures, boosting soil temperature with mulches or IRT plastic sheeting. Winter lows drop to –20°F/–29°C, with occasional extremes to –60°F/–51°C.

ZONE A2. The Intermediate Climate of Anchorage and Cook Inlet

Growing season: mid-May to mid-Sept. Climate is moderated by mountains to the north and south, also by water of Cook Inlet. Microclimates reign supreme: winter lows may be 5°F/–15°C but with extremes of –40°F/–40°C possible. Summer days are cool to mild and frequently cloudy.

ZONE A3. Mild Southern Maritime Climate from Kodiak to Juneau

Growing season: mid-May to Oct. Summers are cool and cloudy, winters rainy and windy. Typical lows are to 18°F/–8°C with extremes to –18°F/–28°C. Winter-spring freeze-thaw cycles damage plants that break growth early. Cool-weather plants revel in climate but annual types mature more slowly than usual.

ZONE H1. Cooler Volcanic Slopes from 2,000 to 5,000 Feet

Found only on Hawaii and Maui, this zone offers cooler air (and cooler nights) than lower Zone H2; temperatures here are better for low-chill fruits (especially at higher elevations) and many non-tropical ornamentals. Warm-season highs reach 65° to 80°F/19° to 27°C; cool-season lows drop to around 45°F/7°C.

ZONE H2. Sea Level to 2,000 Feet: the Coconut Palm Belt

The most heavily populated region in the islands, this has a tepid climate with high temperatures in the 80° to 90°F/27° to 32°C range, low temperatures only to about 65°F/18°C. Rainiest period is Nov. through March, the remaining months, on leeward sides, being relatively dry. Windward sides of islands get more precipitation than leeward sides from passing storms and year-round tradewind showers.

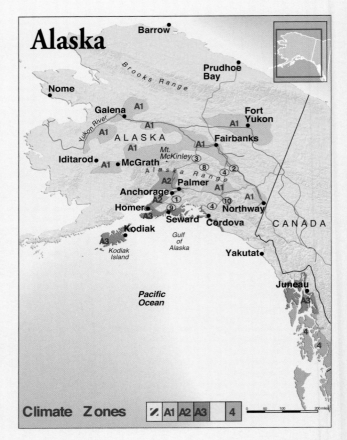

Note: Page references in **bold** type indicate Tropical Sampler entries and usually include a photograph. Page references in *italic* type refer to additional photographs or illustrations.

Abutilon, 39, 43
Abyssinian banana. *See Ensete ventricosum*
Acalypha, 19, 39, **88**
Acanthus mollis, 25
Actinidia kolomikta, 24, *24*
Adam's needle, 22, 25
Aesculus, 23, 44
African daisy. *See Osteospermum*
Agapanthus, 45
Agave, 19, *28–29, 31,* 39, *40, 41, 42,* 44, *44, 48,* **88,** 119, *119.*
    See also Century plant
Ageratum houstonianum. See Floss flower
Aglaonema modestum, 50, 67
Agropyron, 23
Albizia julibrissin, 23
Allamanda, 19, *36,* 43, **88**
Alocasia, 19, 39, *39,* 44, **89**
Aloe, 9, 50, 52, **89,** 119
Alstroemeria aurea, 25
Alternanthera, 18, 39, **90**
Amaranthus (amaranth), 18, *18, 33,* 90
Amaryllis, 35, *35,* 50, *65*
Amazon lily, **102**
Amethyst flower, 18
Angelica tree, 23
Angel's trumpet. *See Brugmansia; Datura*
Anise tree, 24
Anthurium, 35, *35,* 39, 50, **90**
Antigonon leptopus, 18, **90**
Aphelandra squarrosa, 19, 50, 51, **91**
Aporocactus flagelliformis, 51, 52
Arachniodes simplicior (holly fern), *14*
Aralia elata, 23
Araucaria heterophylla, 50, 51
Aristolochia, 43
Asparagus, ornamental, 50
Aspidistra elatior, 25
Aucuba japonica (Japanese aucuba), 24

Bamboo, 9, *9,* 22, *31,* 42, **91**
Bambusa, 42
Banana. *See Musa*
Barleria cristata, 19
Beard tongue, 25
Bear's breech, 25
Begonia, 18, 19, 25, *33,* 44, 50, *50,* 51, *68, 79,* **92**
Bergenia cordifolia, 25
Bignonia capreolata, 24
Bird of paradise. *See Strelitzia reginae*
Black-eyed Susan vine, 18, 120
Blackfoot daisy, 18
Black locust, 23
Blanket flower, 45
Blechnum, 42
Bloodleaf. *See Alternanthera; Iresine*
Blue marguerite, 45
Blue wheatgrass, *23*
Bougainvillea, 14, 19, *28–29, 33, 35, 36,* 39, 43, *43, 79,* **93**

Brazilian plume flower, 79, 108
Breynia nivosa, 6, 39, **93**
Bromeliads, *6,* 19, 35, 39, 42, *44, 48,* 50, 51, *58,* 64, *64,* **94–95,** *94,* 119
Bronze dracaena, 42
Browallia, 18
Brugmansia, 6, 33, *34,* 35, 39, 79, *80,* **95,** 101
Buddleja davidii, 24, *24, 41*
Bugbane, 25
Bulbs, 30, 81–82, *81*
Busy Lizzie, 18, 51
Butterfly bush. *See Buddleja davidii; Clerodendrum*
Butterfly lily. *See Hedychium*

Cacti, *15,* 50, 51, 52, *62,* 119, *119*
Caladium bicolor, 11, 18, *20, 24,* 39, 44, *44, 75, 79,* **96**
Calathea makoyana, 50
Calico plant. *See Alternanthera; Amaranthus; Iresine*
Calla lily, *58*
Camellia, 24, 65
Campsis radicans, 24
Canary bird flower, 19
Candle bush, 35, 44, 117
Canna, 6–7, 17, 19, *20–21, 28,* 30, 35, *37,* 39, *39,* 44, 45, *49, 81,* **96**
Capsicum, 18
Cardinal climber, 107
Cardinal flower, 9, 25
Caribbean copper plant, 103
Caricature plant, 19, *19,* 39, **105**
Carolina jessamine, 24
Cast-iron plant, 25
Castor bean. *See Ricinus communis*
Catalpa bignonioides, 23, 77
Cat whiskers, 35, **111**
Celosia, 18
Century plant, *28–29,* 39, 42, 88, *88*
Chenille plant, 19, 88
Chilean jasmine, 109
Chinese banyan, 104
Chinese evergreen, 50, 67
Chinese hibiscus, 19, 22, 106, *106*
Chlorophytum comosum, 50, 51, **96**
Christmas cactus, *62*
Cigar plant, 39, 100, *100*
Cimicifuga, 25
Cissus, 43
Citrus, 44, **97**
Cleome hasslerana, 18
Clerodendrum, 19, 43, **97**
Climate zones, 14–17, 122–123, *124–126,* 126
Clock vine, 120
Cockscomb, 18
Codiaeum variegatum 'Pictum', 19, *19,* 39, *39,* 50, 51, **98**
Cold-hardy plants, 20–25, 77, 110, 113
Coleus × hybridus, 6, 8, 17, 18, *30, 32, 33, 38,* 39, *49,* 51, **98**
Colocasia, 19, 39, 44, 76, *79,* **89**
Colors, 7, 10–11, 32–39, 45
Common trumpet creeper, 24
Confederate rose, 106
Container gardens, *16,* 30, 54–55, *54,* 65–66, 77, *77*

Copper leaf, 88
Coral bells, 20, 25
Coral fountain, 42
Coral tree, 39, 48
Coral vine, 18, **90**
Cordyline, 6, 19, *19,* 39, 42, 51, *99.* See also Ti plant
Coreopsis verticillata (threadleaf coreopsis), 45
Corn plant, 50, 51, 101
Cosmos atrosanguineus (chocolate cosmos), 18
Costus, 19, 42, 44
Cotinus coggygria, 23, 77
Crape myrtle, 23
Crassula, 119
Crinum, 19, 39, 42, **99**
Crocosmia × crocosmiiflora, 25
Crossandra infundibuliformis, 19, **99**
Crossvine, 24
Croton. *See Codiaeum variegatum* 'Pictum'
Crown of thorns, 103
Cuphea, 39, **100**
Cup-of-gold vine, 19
Curry plant, 105
Cycas (cycads), *20,* 42, **100**
Cyclamen, 62
Cymbopogon citratus, 42, **100**
Cyperus, 39, 42, **101**
Cypress vine, 107

Dahlia, 18, 25, *25, 33, 49, 75, 80*
Darmera peltata, 25
Datura, 22, 33, 35, *37,* **101**
Daylily, 45
Design, 10–13, 27–45
Dieffenbachia, 50, 51
Dioon, 42, 100
Dipladenia. See Mandevilla
Diseases, 66, 79
Dolichos lablab, 18
Dracaena, 19, 42, 50, 51, *63,* **101**
Drainage, 55, 64–66, 77
Dragon tree, 101
Dryopteris, 25
Dumb cane, 50, 51
Duranta, 39, 44, **102**

Echeveria, 119
Elephant's ear *(Alocasia, Colocasia esculenta, Xanthosoma),* 19, *28,* 30, 39, *39,* 44, 76, *79,* **89**
Empress tree, 23, *23,* 77
Ensete ventricosum, 39, 42, 44, 110
Epiphyllum, 119
Epipremnum pinnatum, 43, 50, 51
Equisetum hyemale, 25
Eryngium, 25
Erythrina, 39, 48
Eucalyptus, 80, **102**
Eucharis × grandiflora (Eucharist lily), 44, **102**
Eucomis bicolor, 39
Eulalia. *See Miscanthus sinensis*
Euonymus, 24
Eupatorium purpureum. See Joe Pye weed
Euphorbia, 25, 39, 42, 50, *65,* **103,** 119

Copper leaf, 88
False heather, 100
Fargesia, 42, 91
Fatsia japonica, 24
Feathertop, 114
Felicia amelloides, 45
Felt plant, 42
Ferns, *8,* 25, *31, 40,* 42, *42,* 44, 49, 50, 51, 65, *68,* **103**
Fertilizing, 66, 78
Fig *(Ficus),* 11, 19, 23, *28,* 39, 43, 44, 50, 51, 55, *84,* **104**
Firecracker flower, 19, **99**
Floss flower, 18, *20–21*
Flowering maple, 39, 43
Flowers, 7, 10–11, 33–35, *35*
Foliage, 8, 10–11, *28–29,* 30, 31, 39, 44, 45
Fountain grass. *See Pennisetum*
Fragrance, 7, 10, 34
Frangipani, 35, 42, **115**
Fruits, 9, 11

Gaillardia × grandiflora, 45
Gardenia augusta, 19, 39, **104**
Gelsemium sempervirens, 24
Geranium, *34, 40, 48*
Giant dracaena, 99
Ginger. *See Zingiberaceae*
Ginger lily. *See Hedychium*
Glorybower vine, 19, 97, *97*
Golden creeping daisy, 39
Golden dewdrop, **102**
Golden elderberry, 77
Goldenrain tree, 23
Golden wonder senna, 79
Goldie's wood fern, 25
Gold vein plant, 35, 39, 44, **116**
Grape ivy, 43
Graptophyllum pictum, 19, *19,* 39, **105**
Grasses, ornamental, *32,* 44
Greenhouses, 69–71, *70, 71,* 85, *85*
Gunnera tinctoria, 25
Gynura aurantiaca, 8, 39, 43, 50, **105**

Hardening off, 52, *52*
Heartleaf bergenia, 25
Heavenly bamboo, 24
Hedera, 48, 65, 79
Helichrysum, 8, 40, 43, 44, *44,* **105**
Heliconia, 35, *35,* 42, 44, 79, **106**
Hemerocallis, 45
Heuchera, 20, 25
Hibiscus, 19, 22, *22,* 24, 25, 35, *35, 38,* 39, **106**
Hippeastrum, 35, *35,* 50, *65*
Holly-leaf osmanthus, 24
Honey bush, **109**
Horsetail, 25
Hosta, 20, 25, *25*
Hoya carnosa, 19
Humidity, 64, 70
Hyacinth bean, 18
Hydrangea, 23, 24
Hypericum, 41
Hypoestes phyllostachya, 19

Illicium, 24
Impatiens, 18, *20, 33,* 51, *75*
Indian rhubarb, 25
Indigofera kirilowii (indigo bush), 24

Indoor plants 49–54, *53*, 62–71
Insect pests, 66, 79
Ipomoea, 17, 19, 35, 39, 43, 44, *49,* **107**
Iresine, 19, *28,* 44, *44,* 90, **107**
Ivy, 43, *48,* 65, 71, *79*

Japanese anemone, *31*
Japanese aralia, 24
Japanese coltsfoot, 25
Japanese honeysuckle, 24
Japanese pagoda tree, 23
Jasminum (jasmine), 19, 43, **107**
Jatropha, **108**
Jerusalem cherry, *62,* 118
Joe Pye weed, 20, 25
Joseph's coat. *See Alternanthera;*
   Amaranthus; Iresine
Justicia, 19, 79, **108**

Kalanchoe, 19, 39, 42, 119
Kiwi, 24, *24*
Kniphofia (red-hot poker), 20, *21,* 25
Koelreuteria paniculata, 23

Laburnum × *watereri,* 23
Lady of the night, 51
Lagerstroemia indica, 23
Lantana, 34, 37, **108**
Layering, 41, 56
Lemon grass, 42, **100**
Licorice plant, *8, 40,* 43, 44, *44,* **105**
Lights, supplemental, 67, 85
Ligularia, 20, *21,* 25
Lily-of-the-Nile, 45
Lily-of-the-valley shrub, 24
Liriope muscari (lily turf), 25
Lobelia cardinalis, 9, 25
Lobster-claw. *See Heliconia*
Lonicera japonica, 24
Lotus, 35

Macleaya cordata, 25, *25*
Magnolia, 22, 23, *23,* 35
Mahonia aquifolium, 24
Maintenance, 50, 74–80
Mandevilla, 19, 35, 43, *48,* **109**
Maranta leuconeura, 50
Maternity plant, 42
Melampodium leucanthum, 18
Melianthus major, **109**
Mexican flame vine, 35, 43
Mexican hat, 45
Mexican sunflower, 18, *20–21,* 41
Microclimates, 13
Milkbush, 103
Miscanthus sinensis, 25, *44, 48*
Monstera deliciosa, 19, 50
Montbretia, 25
Moonflower, 35, 107, *107*
Morning glory, **107**
Moses-in-the-cradle, 121
Mulching, 55, 76, 77, 78, 83, *83*
Musa, 11, 19, *20,* 23, *32, 33,* 35, 39, 44, *84,* **110**

Nandina domestica, 24
Naranjilla, 44
Nasturtium. *See Tropaeolum*
Nelumbo, 35

Nerium oleander, 43
New Zealand flax, 42, 45
Nicotiana, 33
Norfolk Island pine, 50, 51
Nurseries, 59

Oleander, 43
Opuntia, 15
Orange clock vine, 120
Orchids, 19, 50, 51, *63,* 65–66, *69, 70, 71,* **111**
Orchid vine, 43
Oregon grape, 24
Orthosiphon stamenis, 35, **111**
Osmanthus heterophyllus, 24
Osteospermum, 37, 39, 44, 45, **112**
Oxalis vulcanicola, 39, 44
Oxydendrum arboreum, 23

Pachystachys lutea, 19, *19, 63,* 108
Pagoda flower, 97
Palm grass, *31*
Palms, 10, *14, 19,* 22, *32,* 42, 49, 50, 51, *52, 67, 69, 79,* **112–113**
Papyrus, 42, **101**
Parrotleaf, 90, *90*
Passion vine *(Passiflora), 9, 9,* 35, 43, *48,* **114**
Paulownia tomentosa, 23, *23,* 77
Peace lily, 50, *50,* 67
Peacock plant, 50
Pelargonium, 34, 40, 48
Pennisetum, 8, 20–21, 42, *49,* **114**
Penstemon, 25, 45
Pentas lanceolata, 18, 35, **114**
Pepper, 18
Peregrina, 108, *108*
Periwinkle, 43
Persian shield, 19, *32,* 39, 80, **119**
Petasites japonicus, 25
Petrea volubilis, 19
Philippine violet, 19
Philodendron, 19, 43, 44, *44,* 50, 51, *55, 65*
Phormium, 30, 33, 42, 45, **115**
Phyllostachys, 42, 91, *91*
Pieris japonica, 24
Pigeon berry, **102**
Pineapple flower, 39
Pine cone ginger, 34, 39, 44, 121
Plantain lily. *See Hosta*
Planting, 54–56, 58, 74–77, 81
Platycerium bifurcatum, 42
Plectranthus, 39, 44
Plumbago, 43
Plume poppy, 25, *25*
Plumeria, 35, 42, **115**
Poinsettia, *65*
Poisonous plants, 101, 116
Polka-dot plant, 19
Pools and ponds, 12, 13
Portulaca, 18
Potato vine, 39, 43, 118, *118*
Pothos, 43, 50, 51
Prayer plant, 50
Princess flower, 19, *32,* 35, 120, *120*
Propagation, 56–59, *56, 57,* 81–83, *81, 82*
Pruning, 55, 74, 77, 79, 80
Pseuderanthemum atropurpureum, 39
Purple heart, 121

Purple passion vine, purple velvet
   plant. *See Gynura aurantiaca*

Queen palm, 42
Queen sago, 100
Queen's tears. *See* Bromeliads
Queen's wreath, 19, **90**

Ratibida columnifera, 45
Ravenala madagascariensis, 30, 42
Red buckeye, 23
Red horsechestnut, 23
Red-hot poker, 20, *21,* 25
Rheum × *hybridum,* 25
Rhipsalidopsis, 119
Rhododendron, 19, 24, 65
Rhubarb, 25
Rhus typhina, 24
Ricinus communis, 10, 18, *18, 20–21, 30, 33,* 41, 44, **116**
Robinia pseudoacacia, 23
Rosa, 45
Rose-mallow, 22, *22,* 25, 35, *35,* 106
Rose moss. *See Portulaca*
Rose of Sharon, 22, 24, 106
Rubber tree, 19, *28,* 39, 44, 50, 51, 55, 104
Russelia equisetiformis, 42

Saccharum officinarum, 42
Sage *(Salvia), 6–7,* 18, *18, 30,* 35, 75
Sago palm, *20,* 100, *100*
Sambucus canadensis, 77
Sanchezia speciosa, 35, 39, 44, **116**
Sansevieria trifasciata, 19, 42, 50, 51, **117**
Schefflera, 50, 51
Schlumbergera, 62, 119
Sea holly, 25
Sedum, 20, 25, *33, 41,* 52, 119
Senecio confusus, 35, 43
Senna, 35, 44, 79, **117**
Setaria palmifolia, 31
Shade, 52–54, *53,* 69, 70
Shell ginger, 35, 39, 42, *58*
Shrimp plant, 19, 79, 108, *108*
Silk tree, 23
Silver dollar tree, 80, 102, *102*
Silver vase plant, 39, 42, 94
Sky flower *(Duranta),* 39, 44, **102**
Sky flower *(Thunbergia),* 120, *120*
Smoke tree, 23, 77
Snail vine, 43
Snake plant, 19, 42, 50, 51, **117**
Snow bush, *6,* 39, **93**
Snow-on-the-mountain, 103
Soapweed, 22, 25
Soil, 65–66, 74–75, 77
Solandra maxima, 19
Solanum, 35, 39, 43, 44, *62,* **118**
Sophora japonica, 23
Sourwood, 23
Spathe flower. *See Anthurium*
Spathiphyllum wallisii, 50, *50,* 67
Spider flower, 18
Spider plant, 50, 51, **96**
Spiderwort, 121, *121*
Spiral flag, 42, 44
Split-leaf philodendron, 19, 50
Staghorn sumac, 24

Star clusters. *See Pentas lanceolata*
Stigmaphyllon ciliatum, 43
Stonecrop. *See Sedum*
Strap flower, 90
Strelitzia reginae, 19, 35, 42, *42,* 44, 76, **118**
Strobilanthes dyeranus, 19, *32,* 39, 80, **119**
Subtropical plants, 11, 15, 22
Succulents, *40,* 50, *58, 68,* **119**
Sugar cane, 32, 42
Sunrooms, 68–69, *68, 69*
Sweet potato, ornamental, *17,* 19, 39, 44, *49,* 107
Syagrus romanzoffianum, 42

Taro *(Alocasia, Colocasia esculenta, Xanthosoma),* **89**
Texas star, 25
Thorn apple *(Datura),* 35, **101**
Thunbergia, 18, 35, 43, **120**
Tibouchina, 19, *32,* 35, **120**
Ti plant, *6,* 19, *19,* 39, 42, 51, 99, *99*
Tithonia rotundifolia, 18, *20,* 41
Torenia fournieri, 18, 33, 51
Tradescantia, 19, 39, 44, 50, 51, *66,* **121**
Traveler's tree, *30,* 42
Tropaeolum (nasturtium), 11, 18, 19, 52

Umbrella plant, 39, **101**

Verbena, 8, 45
Viburnum rhytidophyllum, 24, *24*
Vigna caracalla, 43
Vinca major, 43

Wandering Jew, 50, 51, 66, 121
Watering, 64, 69, 71, 76, 78
Wax flower, 19
Wedelia trilobata, 39
Wind protection, 13
Winter care, 13, 62–65, 68, 70–71, 81–85, *82, 83, 84, 85*
Wishbone flower, 18, 51
Wisteria, 24
Wood fern, 25
Wood sorrel, 39, 44

Xanthosoma, 39, 44, **89**

Yellow shrimp plant, 19, *19, 63,* 108
Yucca, 22, 25, 119

Zantedeschia rehmanii, 58
Zebra plant, 19, 50, 51, **91**
Zingiberaceae, 11, 18, 19, *19,* 34, 35, 39, 42, 44, *58,* 79, **121**